Over and Over Again
Poems and songs for the very young

Over and Over Again

Poems and songs for the very young

Barbara Ireson and Christopher Rowe

Illustrated by Russell Coulson

Hutchinson
London Melbourne Sydney Auckland Johannesburg

For Sarah and Lucy

Hutchinson Children's Books Ltd

An imprint of the Hutchinson Publishing Group

17–21 Conway Street, London W1P 6JD

Hutchinson Publishing Group (Australia) Pty Ltd
PO Box 496, 16–22 Church Street, Hawthorne, Melbourne,
Victoria 3122

Hutchinson Group (NZ) Ltd
32–34 View Road, PO Box 40-086, Glenfield, Auckland 10

Hutchinson Group (SA) Pty Ltd
PO Box 337, Bergvlei 2012, South Africa

First published by Beaver Books 1978
Hutchinson edition 1984

Text © Barbara Ireson and Christopher Rowe 1978

Illustrations © Hamlyn Publishing Group Ltd 1978

Music of original songs © Christopher Rowe 1978

Printed and bound in Great Britain by
Anchor Brendon Ltd, Tiptree, Essex

ISBN 0 09 156740 8

Contents

O where, O where has my little dog gone?	7
Talking tick tock talk	45
Look at your hat!	61
Clickety-click and clickety-clack	79
Wibbleton to Wobbleton	115
Round and round the village	135
One-eyed Jack and Peg-leg Pete	181
Index and list of copyright holders	218

O where, O where has my little dog gone?

O where, O where has my little dog gone?

O where, O where has my little dog gone?
O where, O where can he be?
With his ears cut short and his tail cut long,
O where, O where can he be?

Little man, little man

Little man, little man,
Where is your house?
My house is a hole,
For I am a MOUSE.

Where have you been?

Where have you been?
I've been to the zoo,
I saw a monkey and thought it was you.

Where have you been?
I've been there too,
And I saw a baboon who looked just like you.

The five little pigs

This little pig went to market;
This little pig stayed at home;
This little pig had roast beef;
This little pig had none;
This little pig cried 'Wee, wee, wee!
I can't find my way home.'

If I had a donkey

If I had a donkey
   And he wouldn't go,
Do you think I'd wallop him?
   Oh, no, no!

I'd put him in the barn
   And give him some corn,
The best little donkey
   That ever was born.

Up in the North

Up in the North, a long way off,
The donkey's got the whooping cough;
He whooped so hard with the whooping cough,
He whooped his head and his tail right off!

Little Robin Redbreast

Little Robin Redbreast
   Sat upon a rail,
Niddle noddle went his head
And wag went his tail!

Jack and Jill

There were two little dickey birds sitting on a hill,
One named Jack and the other named Jill.
Fly away, Jack. Fly away, Jill.
Come back, Jack. Come back, Jill.

In my little bed

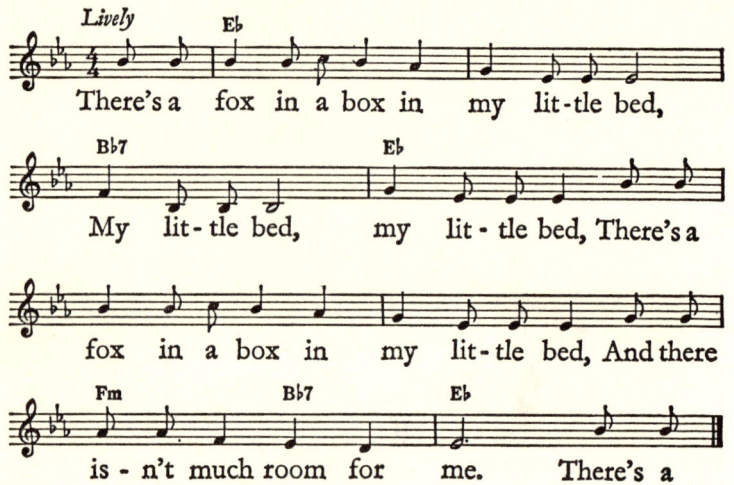

There's a fox in a box in my little bed,
My little bed, my little bed,
There's a fox in a box in my little bed,
And there isn't much room for me.

There's a goat in a coat in my little bed ...

There's a snake in a cake in my little bed ...

There's a pup in a cup in my little bed ...

There's a lamb in some jam in my little bed ...

There's a mouse in a house in my little bed ...

There's a bear in a chair in my little bed ...

Ladybird, ladybird

Ladybird, ladybird, fly away home!
Your house in on fire, your children are gone.

All but one, and her name is Ann,
And she crept under the frying pan.

O ladybird, ladybird, fly away home!
Your house is on fire, your children are gone.

There was a small maiden named Maggie

There was a small maiden named Maggie,
Whose dog was enormous and shaggy;
  The front end of him
    Looked vicious and grim –
But the tail end was friendly and waggy!

I'm a pet

I'm a pet
And yet
If I don't know you
I'll throw you –
>I'm a horse,
>Of course.

In the garden

The dog was on the log,
The cat was on the mat,
The thrush was in the bush,
The bee was in the tree,
And everyone in the garden
>Was happy.

I wish I were a lamb in the field

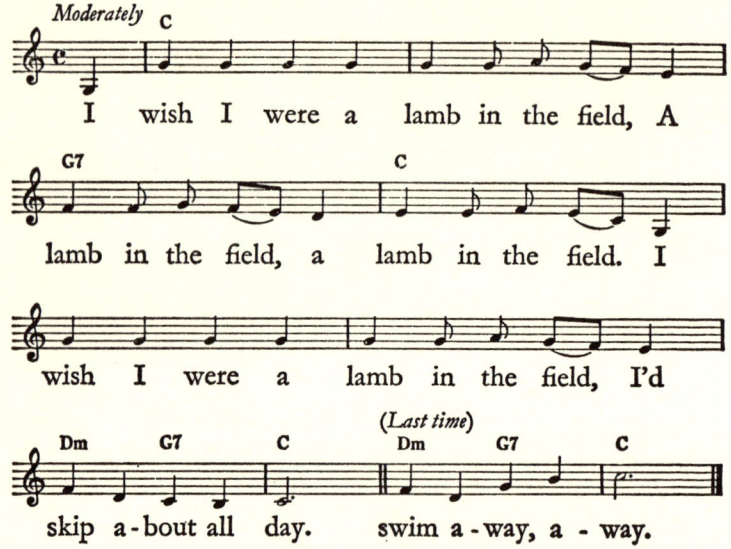

I wish I were a lamb in the field,
A lamb in the field, a lamb in the field.
I wish I were a lamb in the field,
I'd skip about all day.

I wish I were a horse in the stable,
A horse in the stable, a horse in the stable.
I wish I were a horse in the stable,
I'd munch and munch my hay.

I wish I were a fish in the sea,
A fish in the sea, a fish in the sea.
I wish I were a fish in the sea,
I'd swim away, away.

Eency, weency spider

Eency, weency spider went up the water spout,
Down came the rain and washed the spider out.
Out came the sun and dried up all the rain,
And the eency, weency spider went up the spout again.

A frog went walking on a summer's day

A frog went walk-ing on a sum-mer's day, A-hum, a-hum. A frog went walk-ing on a sum-mer's day, He met Miss Mous-ie on the way, A-hum, a-hum, a-hum, a-hum, a-hum.

A frog went walking on a summer's day,
   A-hum, a-hum.
A frog went walking on a summer's day,
He met Miss Mousie on the way,
   A-hum, a-hum, a-hum, a-hum, a-hum.

He said, 'Miss Mousie, will you marry me?'
   A-hum, a-hum.
He said, 'Miss Mousie, will you marry me?
We'll live together in an apple tree.'
   A-hum, a-hum, a-hum, a-hum, a-hum.

The first to the wedding was Mr Dick,
   A-hum, a-hum.
The first to the wedding was Mr Dick;
He ate so much he nearly got sick.
   A-hum, a-hum, a-hum, a-hum, a-hum.

And what do you think they had for supper?
   A-hum, a-hum.
And what do you think they had for supper?
A fried mosquito and bread and butter.
A-hum, a-hum, a-hum, a-hum, a-hum.

And what do you think they had on the shelf?
   A-hum, a-hum.
And what do you think they had on the shelf?
If you want to know, go look for yourself.
   A-hum, a-hum, a-hum, a-hum, a-hum.

The lion is king of the jungle

The lion is king of the jungle,
A terrible beast to behold;
All of the animals know who he is,
And everyone does as he's told,
Yes, everyone does as he's told.

There's no-one as strong as the lion,
And this is why he is so proud:
He leaps in the air and he creeps through the grass,
And his voice is terribly loud,
Yes, his voice is terribly loud.

You know when the lion is angry,
He lets out a frightening roar;
The birds fly away and the animals hide,
They know that he's coming for sure,
Yes, they know that he's coming for sure.

The lion is frightened of no-one,
He walks with his head held high;
The animals know by the mane on his neck
That this is the king going by,
Yes, this is the king going by.

The lion is king of the jungle,
A terrible beast to behold;
All of the animals know who he is,
And everyone does as he's told,
Yes, everyone does as he's told.

The sheep and the wolf

Sheep, sheep, come home!

We are afraid.

What are you afraid of?

The wolf.

The wolf's not been here –
He's not been near
For many a year,
So sheep, sheep, come home!

Sheep, sheep, come home!

We are afraid.

What are you afraid of?

The lion.

The lion's not been here –
He's not been near
For many a year,
So sheep, sheep, come home!

Sheep, sheep, come home!

We are afraid.

What are you afraid of?

The tiger.

The tiger's not been here –
He's not been near
For many a year,
So sheep, sheep, come home!

If you should ever need a hole

If you should ever need a hole
Just go and find a small black mole.
He'll dig and dig
Until it's big,
But if you don't stop this clever digger,
You'll see your hole get bigger and BIGGER!

Hey diddle diddle

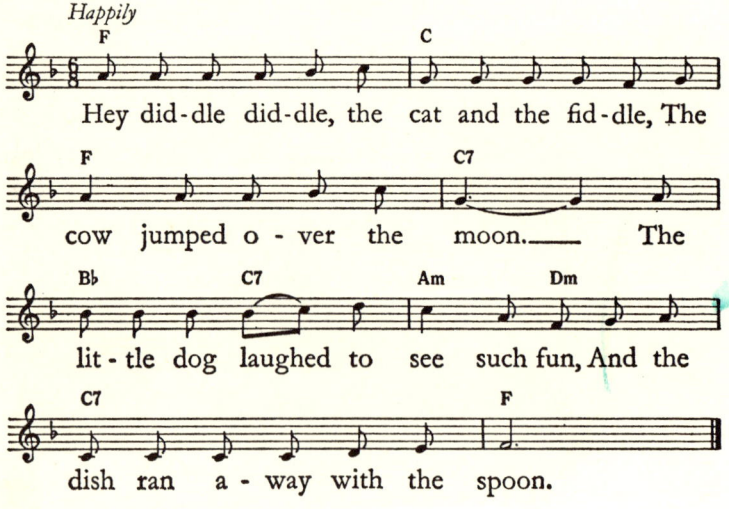

Hey diddle diddle, the cat and the fiddle,
The cow jumped over the moon.
The little dog laughed to see such fun,
And the dish ran away with the spoon.

Baa, baa, black sheep

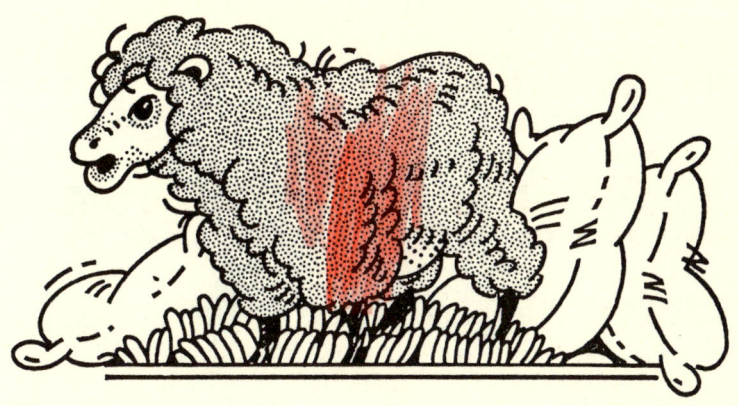

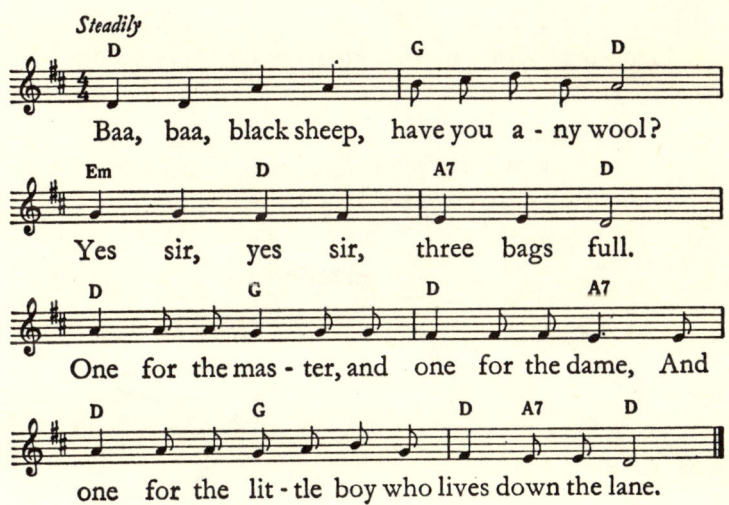

Baa, baa, black sheep, have you any wool?
Yes sir, yes sir, three bags full.
One for the master, and one for the dame,
And one for the little boy who lives down the lane.

The north wind doth blow

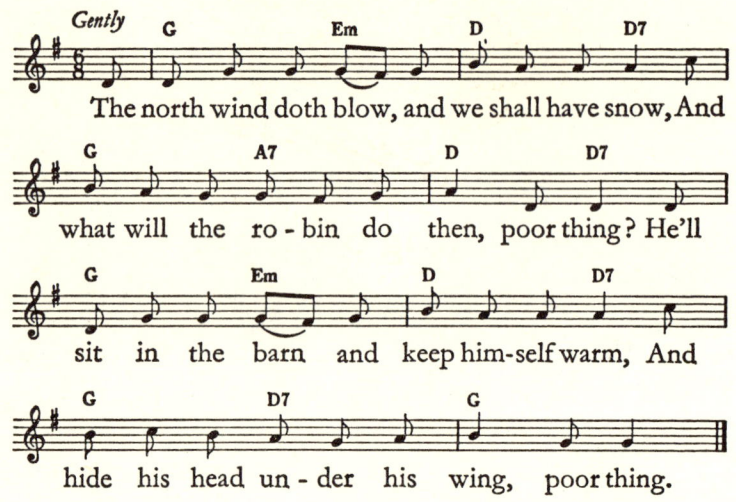

The north wind doth blow, and we shall have snow, And what will the ro-bin do then, poor thing? He'll sit in the barn and keep him-self warm, And hide his head un-der his wing, poor thing.

The north wind doth blow, and we shall have snow,
And what will the robin do then, poor thing?
He'll sit in the barn and keep himself warm,
And hide his head under his wing, poor thing.

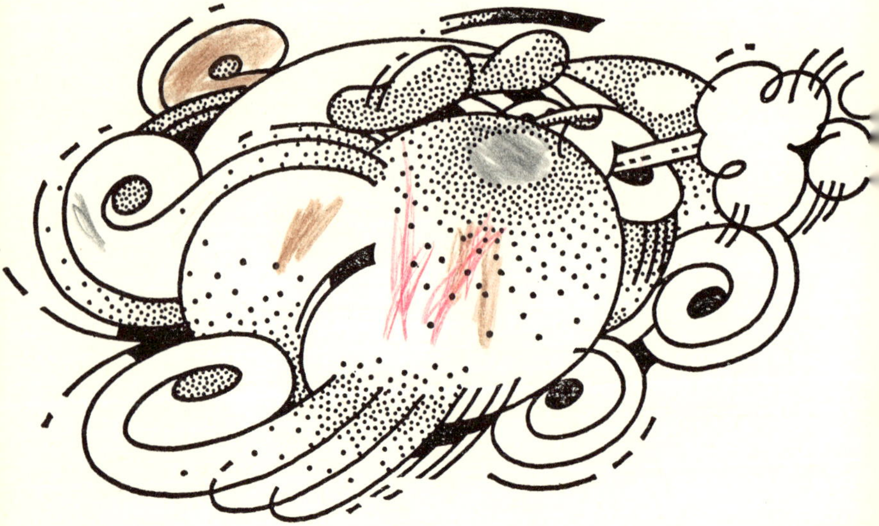

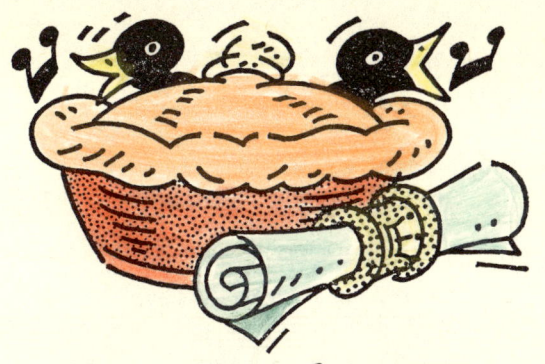

Sing a song of sixpence

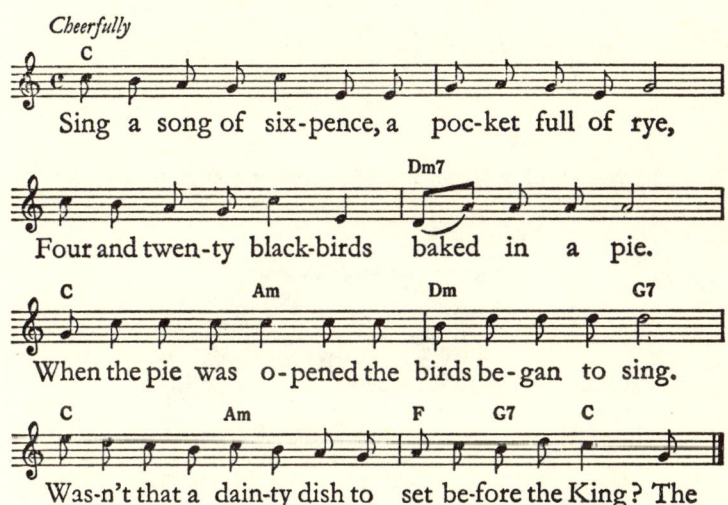

Sing a song of sixpence, a pocket full of rye,
Four and twenty blackbirds baked in a pie.
When the pie was opened the birds began to sing.
Wasn't that a dainty dish to set before the King?

The King was in his counting-house counting out his money;
The Queen was in the parlour eating bread and honey;
The maid was in the garden hanging out the clothes.
Down came a blackbird and pecked off her nose!

Would you dare?

Would you dare, would you dare
To dance round the room with a big shaggy bear?

Will you try, will you try
To wipe a tear from an elephant's eye?

Could you smile, could you smile
As you sat on the back of a long crocodile?

Would you ever, would you ever
Tickle a lion with a yellow feather?

Will you make, will you make
Friends with a slithering ten foot long snake?

Three blind mice

Three blind mice, three blind mice,
See how they run, see how they run;
They all ran after the farmer's wife,
Who cut off their tails with a carving knife,
Did you ever see such a thing in your life
As three blind mice!

Five pigeons

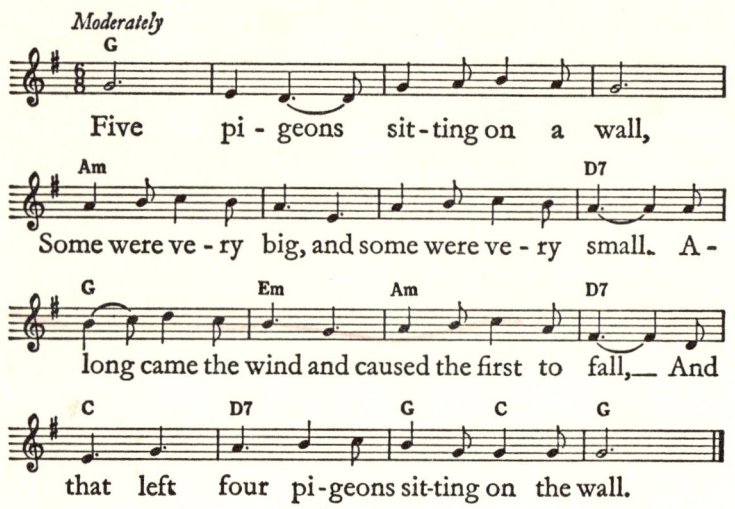

Five pi-geons sit-ting on a wall, Some were ve-ry big, and some were ve-ry small. A-long came the wind and caused the first to fall,— And that left four pi-geons sit-ting on the wall.

Five pigeons sitting on a wall,
Some were very big, and some were very small.
Along came the wind and caused the first to fall,
And that left four pigeons sitting on the wall.

Four pigeons sitting on a wall,
Some were very big, and some were very small.
Along came the wind and caused the next to fall,
And that left three pigeons sitting on the wall.

Three pigeons sitting on a wall,
Some were very big, and some were very small.
Along came the wind and caused the next to fall,
And that left two pigeons sitting on the wall.

Two pigeons sitting on a wall,
One was very big and one was very small.
Along came the wind and caused one more to fall,
And that left one pigeon sitting on the wall.

One pigeon sitting on a wall,
Left on his own with no-one else at all.
Along came the wind, and he didn't want to fall,
So off he flew – and that meant there was no-one on the wall!

Who is that?

Rat a tat tat, who is that?
Only grandma's pussy cat.
What do you want?
A pint of milk.
Where's your money?
In my pocket.
Where's your pocket?
I forgot it.

Oh you silly pussy cat!

In the forest

I'm a lion in the forest
And I'm looking for my tea.
OH PLEASE MR LION,
DON'T EAT ME!

I'm a lion in the forest
And I must have some meat.
OH PLEASE MR LION,
I'M NOT THE ONE TO EAT!

I'm a lion in the forest,
I've waited long enough.
OH NO, MR LION!
YOU'D FIND ME VERY TOUGH!

I love little pussy

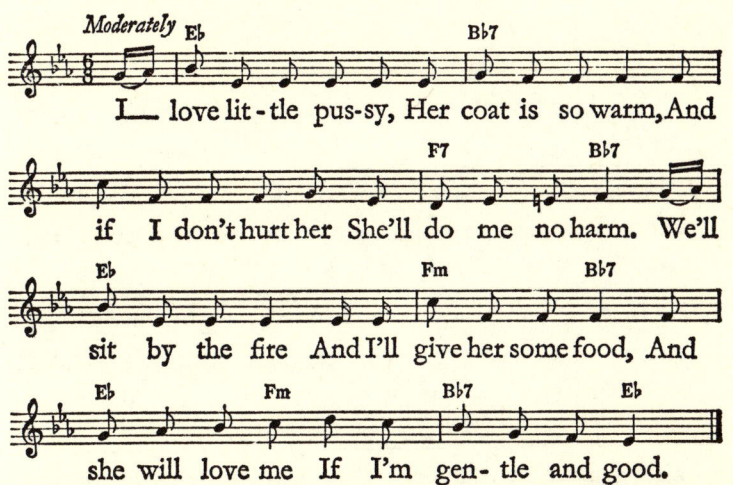

I love little pussy,
   Her coat is so warm,
And if I don't hurt her
   She'll do me no harm.

We'll sit by the fire
   And I'll give her some food,
And she will love me
   If I'm gentle and good.

The bear went over the mountain

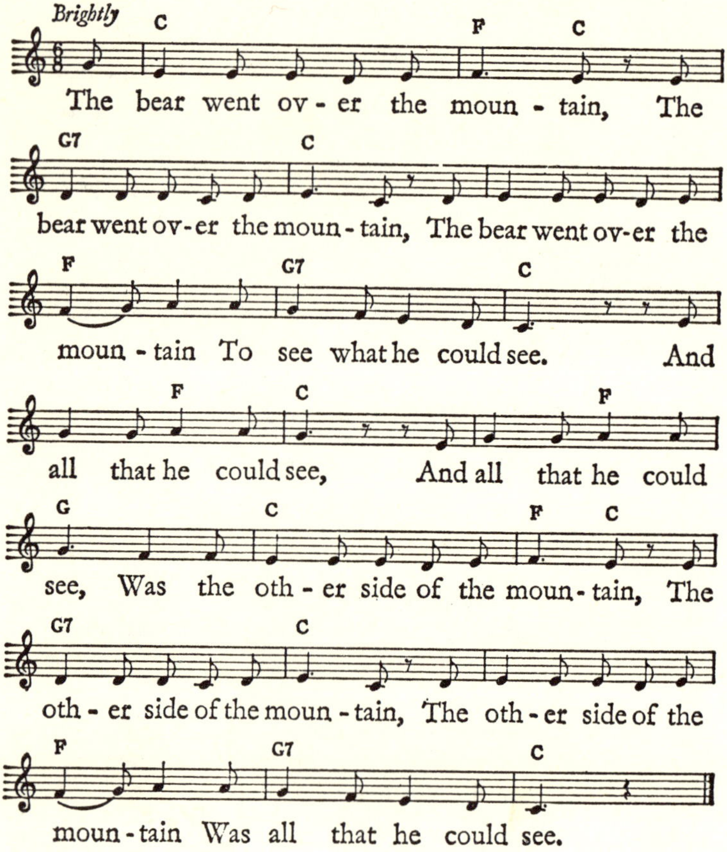
Brightly
C F C
The bear went ov - er the moun - tain, The
G7 C
bear went ov - er the moun - tain, The bear went ov - er the
F G7 C
moun - tain To see what he could see. And
F C F
all that he could see, And all that he could
G C F C
see, Was the oth - er side of the moun - tain, The
G7 C
oth - er side of the moun - tain, The oth - er side of the
F G7 C
moun - tain Was all that he could see.

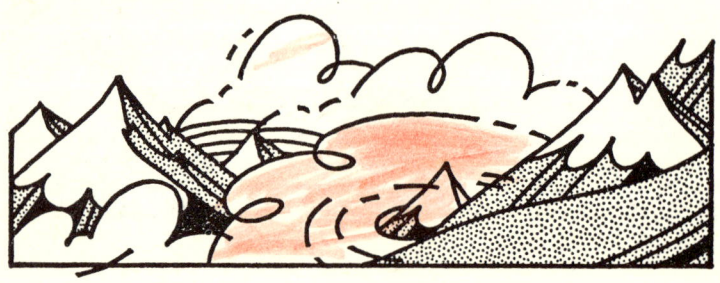

The bear went over the mountain,
The bear went over the mountain,
The bear went over the mountain
To see what he could see.
And all that he could see,
And all that he could see,
Was the other side of the mountain,
The other side of the mountain,
The other side of the mountain
Was all that he could see.

I went for a walk in the park

I went for a walk in the park today,
And who do you think I met on the way?

I met a lion, and what did he say...?
ROAR, ROAR, ROAR.

I went for a walk in the park today,
And who do you think I met on the way?

I met an elephant, and what did he say...?
TRUMPETY, TRUMPETY, TRUMPETY.

I went for a walk in the park today,
And who do you think I met on the way?

I met a snake, and what did he say...?
SSSSS, SSSSS, SSSSS.

Six little ducks

Six little ducks that I once knew,
Fat ones, skinny ones they were too;
But the one little duck with the feathers on his back,
He ruled the others with his 'Quack, quack, quack!
        quack, quack, quack!'
He ruled the others with his 'Quack, quack, quack!'

Down the river they would go,
Wibble, wabble, wibble, wabble, to and fro;
But the one little duck with the feathers on his back, *etc.*

Home from the river they would come,
Wibble, wabble, wibble, wabble, ho-hum-hum;
But the one little duck with the feathers on his back, *etc.*

Cock Robin

Who killed Cock Robin?
'I,' said the sparrow,
'With my bow and arrow,
I killed Cock Robin.'

Chorus *All the birds of the air*
Fell a-sighing and a-sobbing
When they heard of the death
Of poor Cock Robin,
When they heard of the death
Of poor Cock Robin.

Who saw him die?
'I,' said the fly,
'With my little eye,
I saw him die.'

Who'll toll the bell?
'I,' said the bull,
'Because I can pull,
I'll toll the bell.'

Who'll dig his grave?
'I,' said the owl,
'With my little trowel,
I'll dig his grave.'

Who'll be his parson?
'I,' said the rook,
'With my bell and book,
I'll be the parson.'

Who'll be chief mourner?
'I,' said the dove,
'I'll mourn for my love,
I'll be chief mourner.'

One elephant

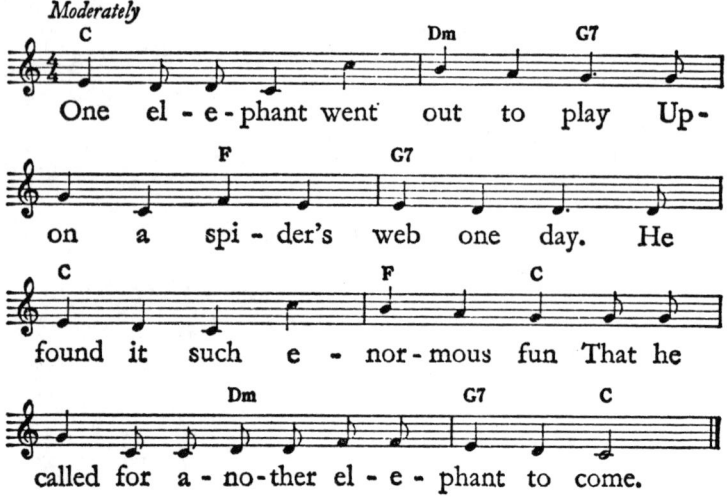

One elephant went out to play
Upon a spider's web one day.
He found it such enormous fun
That he called for another elephant to come.

The boy and the owl

A little boy went into a barn,
  And lay down on some hay;
An owl came out and flew about,
  And the little boy ran away.

Robin Redbreast and Puss

Little Robin Redbreast sat upon a tree,
Up went Pussy-cat and down went he.
Down came Pussy-cat and away Robin ran;
Says little Robin Redbreast, 'Catch me if you can.'

Little Robin Redbreast flew up on the wall,
Pussy-cat jumped after him and almost had a fall.
Little Robin chirped and sang. And what did Pussy say?
Pussy-cat said, 'Mew,' and Robin flew away.

The animals went in two by two

Moderately

The a-ni-mals went in two by two, Hur-rah!— Hur-rah!— The a-ni-mals went in two by two, Hur-rah!— Hur-rah!— The a-ni-mals went in two by two, The e-le-phant and the kan-ga-roo, And they all went in-to the ark For to get out of the rain.—

The animals went in two by two,
Hurrah! Hurrah!
The animals went in two by two,
Hurrah! Hurrah!
The animals went in two by two,
The elephant and the kangaroo,
And they all went into the ark
For to get out of the rain.

The animals went in three by three . . .
The wasp, the ant and the bumblebee . . .

The animals went in four by four . . .
The great hippopotamus stuck in the door . . .

The animals went in five by five . . .
By eating each other they kept alive . . .

The animals went in six by six . . .
They turned out the monkey because of his tricks . . .

The animals went in seven by seven . . .
The little pig thought he was going to heaven . . .

The animals went in eight by eight . . .
The tortoise thought he was going to be late . . .

The animals went in nine by nine . . .
Marching up in a long straight line . . .

The animals went in ten by ten . . .
Last one in was the little red hen . . .

Chook, chook, chook, chook, chook

Chook, chook, chook, chook, chook,
Good morning Mrs Hen.
How many chickens have you got?
Madam, I've got ten.
Four of them are yellow,
Four of them are brown,
Two of them are speckled,
The nicest in the town.
Chook, chook, chook, chook, chook,
Cock-a-doodle-doo!

If

If I could walk on the ceiling
The way that spiders do,
If I could hop for miles and miles
Just like a kangaroo,
If I could fly like a blackbird,
Or swim like a fish in the sea,
I'd be a funny person;
In fact, I wouldn't be me!

Talking tick tock talk

Talking tick tock talk

Repeat final chorus

I'm a clock on the wall looking down on you all,
And I'm talking tick tock talk;
There's nobody who sounds like I do
When I'm talking tick tock talk.
There's a handle on the door and a carpet on the floor,
But they never make a sound like me,
So here I stay passing time away,
Talking tick tock talk.

Chorus Tick tock, tick tock, tick tock, tick tock,
Talking tick tock talk.

Well the kettle can sing and the telephone ring,
But they can't talk tick tock talk;
The curtains hang and the doors go bang,
But they can't talk tick tock talk.
In the middle of the night when you're tucked up tight
And dreaming in your bed,
I won't be asleep, for I just keep
On talking tick tock talk.

Well the water can splash and plates can smash,
But they can't talk tick tock talk;
Well the cleaner can hum and the banjo strum,
But they can't talk tick tock talk.
My hands go round as I make this sound,
And I point to the time of day;
I've a lovely view and nothing to do
But talking tick tock talk.

Well the fire can roar and the milk jug pour,
But they can't talk tick tock talk;
The staircase creaks and the armchair squeaks,
But they can't talk tick tock talk.
And if you're sad I'll make you glad,
You'll feel much better I know
If you listen each day to me chattering away,
Just talking tick tock talk.

I like

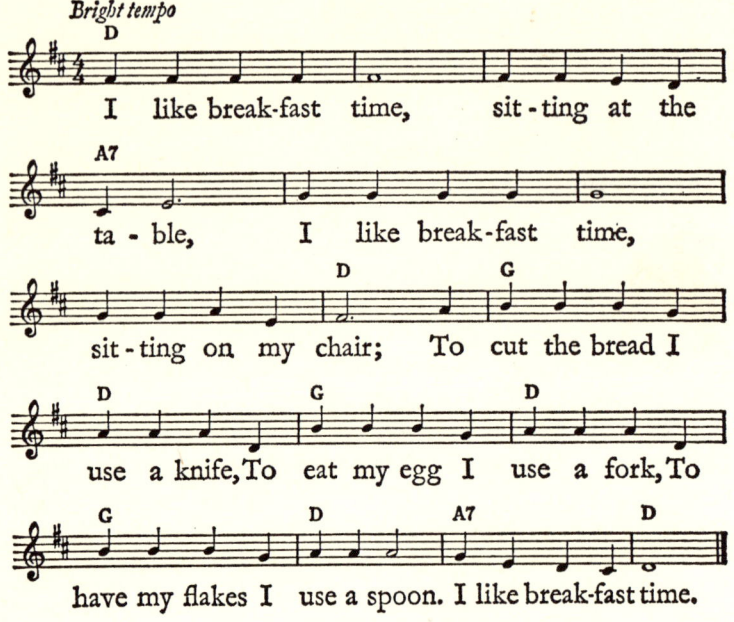

I like breakfast time, sitting at the table,
I like breakfast time, sitting on my chair;
To cut the bread I use a knife,
To eat my egg I use a fork,
To have my flakes I use a spoon.
I like breakfast time.

I like dinner time, sitting at the table,
I like dinner time, sitting on my chair;
To cut the meat I use a knife,
To eat it up I use a fork,
To have my sweet I use a spoon.
I like dinner time.

I like supper time, sitting at the table,
I like supper time, sitting on my chair;
To spread the jam I use a knife,
To eat the ham I use a fork,
To stir my tea I use a spoon.
I like supper time.

Too late

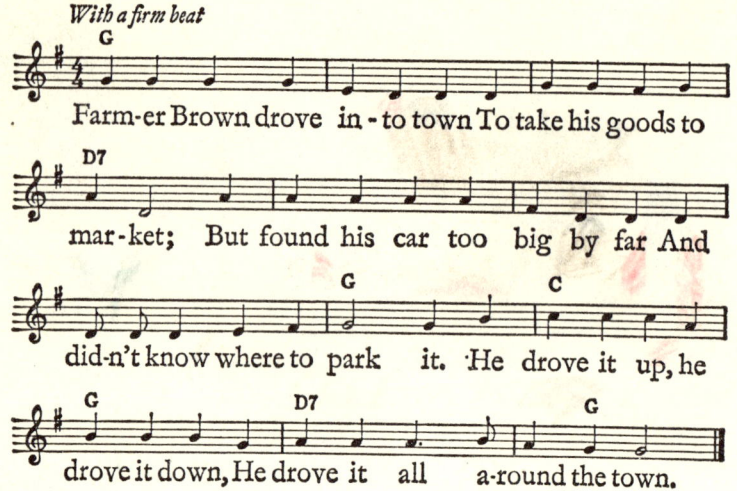

Farmer Brown drove into town
To take his goods to market;
But found his car too big by far
And didn't know where to park it.
He drove it up, he drove it down,
He drove it all around the town.

'I cannot see a place that's free.
It seems they've all been taken,'
He said, as he drove round and round
With all his eggs and bacon.
He drove it up, he drove it down,
He drove it all around the town.

At last he found an empty space
And there he chose to park it;
He took out what he had to sell
And marched off to the market.
He drove it up, he drove it down,
He drove it all around the town.

But sad to state it was too late,
The market now had ended;
And Farmer Brown's ride into town
Was not what he intended.
He drove it up, he drove it down,
He drove it all around the town.

Tired Ben

'I'm going to sleep,' said Tired Ben,
'Don't wake me up till half past ten.'

'Half past ten is far too late,
I'll get you up at half past eight.'

Lazy Mary, will you get up?

Lazy Mary, will you get up,
Will you get up, will you get up?
Lazy Mary, will you get up,
Will you get up today?

No, no, Mother, I won't get up,
I won't get up, I won't get up.
No, no, Mother, I won't get up,
I won't get up today.

There isn't time

There isn't time,
There isn't time
For me to sing
This little rhyme.

I'll say goodbye,
I'll say goodbye
For it is late
And I must fly . . .
          Goodbye.

What's the time?

We all get up at seven
And Daddy leaves at eight,
Then Mummy puts my breakfast egg
With toast upon my plate.

I leave my school at twelve
And Daddy's back at one,
We sit down at the table
And lunchtime has begun.

Six o'clock is suppertime
But Daddy isn't there,
I listen from my bed
For his footsteps on the stair.

Hickory dickory dock

Brightly

Hic-ko-ry dic-ko-ry dock. The
mouse ran up the clock. The
clock struck one, the mouse ran down,
Hic-ko-ry dic-ko-ry dock.

Hickory dickory dock.
The mouse ran up the clock.
The clock struck one, the mouse ran down,
Hickory dickory dock.

The clock stands still

The clock stands still
But the hands go round,
All the time
You hear this sound –
Tick tock, tick tock, tick tock . . .

Time is fun

Time is fun,
See it run.
Clock hands go
Very slow,
Round and round.
What's that sound?
Tock, tick, tock,
Says the clock,
See it run.
Time is fun.

O dear, what can the matter be?

O dear, what can the matter be?
O dear, what can the matter be?
O dear, what can the matter be?
Johnny's so long at the fair.

He promised to buy me a fairing should please me,
And then for a kiss, O he vowed he would tease me.
He promised to buy me a bunch of blue ribbons
To tie up my bonnie brown hair.

O dear, what can the matter be?
O dear, what can the matter be?
O dear, what can the matter be?
Johnny's so long at the fair.

What time is it?

Playtime, playtime,
Best time of the day time.

Lunchtime, lunchtime,
Come and have a munch time.

Teatime, teatime,
Just for you and me time.

Bedtime, bedtime,
Laying down the head time.

What's the time?

What's the time?
Play-time. I'll make a man of clay.
What's the time?
Dinner-time. There's fish to eat today.
What's the time?
Tea-time. I'll put my bricks away.
What's the time?
Bed-time. I've had a busy day.

In the mornings

At seven o'clock the milkman comes,
I hear him slam the gate.
At eight o'clock the postman comes,
And he is never late.
But then I sit on the wall and wait
And I listen for the baker-man.
He's always late; it's half-past eight
Before I hear his van.

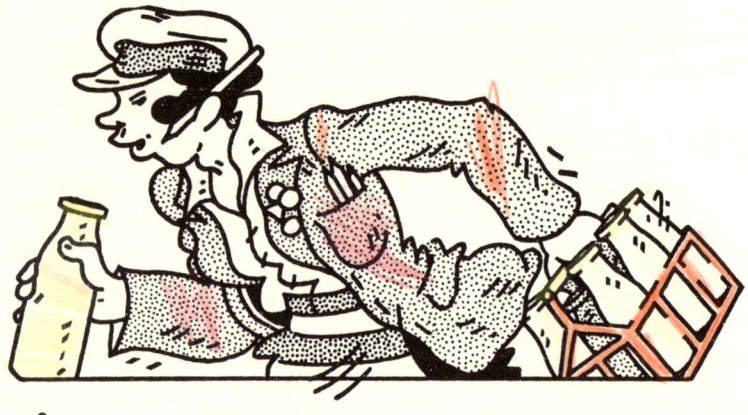

Time and time again

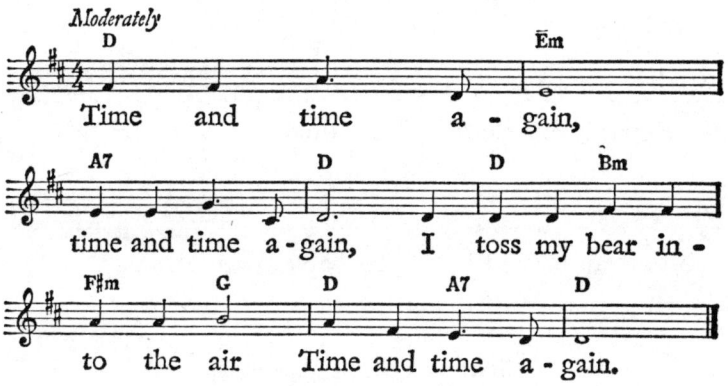

Time and time again, time and time again,
I toss my bear into the air
Time and time again.

Time and time again, time and time again,
I throw my ball against the wall
Time and time again.

Time and time again, time and time again,
I get my boat and make it float
Time and time again.

Time and time again, time and time again,
I fire my gun and off I run
Time and time again.

Mornings

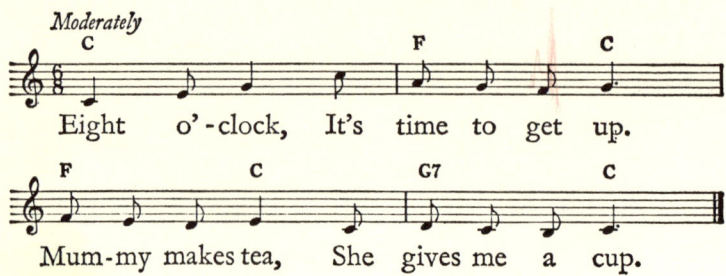

Eight o'clock,
It's time to get up.
Mummy makes tea,
She gives me a cup.

Daddy must leave
At half past eight,
He hurries his breakfast,
He mustn't be late.

And then it's my turn
To hurry away
To the school down the road
Where I go every day.

Look at your hat!

Another me!

When I look into the looking-glass
There's someone I always see.
I stand there staring through at her
And she looks back at me.

I can touch her shiny hair . . . almost.
I can hold her outstretched hand . . . almost.
But she cannot ever pass
Through the silver looking-glass.
Whoever can she be?

In the cupboard

I went to the cupboard
And what did I see?

> One lemon
> Two oranges
> Three apples
> Four pears
> Five peaches
> Six plums
> Seven bananas
> Eight cherries
> Nine gooseberries
> Ten raspberries . . .

And up on the shelf
All by itself –
A BIRTHDAY CAKE FOR ME!

Look at your hat!

Look at your hat!
Just look at your hat!
It's back to front
And squashed quite flat.
Look at your hat!

Look at your shirt!
Just look at your shirt!
It's inside out
And black with dirt.
Look at your shirt!

Look at your dress!
Just look at your dress!
It's rumpled and crumpled
And needs a press.
Look at your dress!

Look at your shoes!
Just look at your shoes!
They're full of holes –
Not fit to use.
Look at your shoes!

Look at your face!
Just look at your face!
It hasn't been washed.
What a disgrace!
Look at your face!

GO HOME

What we want

Jelly and cream, jelly and cream,
What we want is jelly and cream;
We'll eat it for dinner, we'll eat it for tea,
We'll eat it for ever – try us and see!
Jelly and cream, jelly and cream,
That's our favourite, jelly and cream.

Bacon and beans, *etc.*

Sausage and chips, *etc.*

Bangers and mash, *etc.*

Polly put the kettle on

Polly put the kettle on, Polly put the kettle on,
Polly put the kettle on, we'll all have tea.
Sukey take it off again, Sukey take it off again,
Sukey take it off again, they've all gone away!

Father and Mother and Big Brother John

Father and Mother and Big Brother John
Went to market one by one.
Father fell off!
Mother fell off!
But Big Brother John went on and on
And on and on and on.

My Mummy

My Mummy is a Mummy
And she's a teacher too.
When she's not looking after me,
She's teaching kids like you.

My Mummy is a Mummy
And she does sewing too.
When she's not looking after me,
She's making coats for you.

My Mummy is a Mummy
And she's a driver too.
When she's not looking after me,
She drives a coach for you.

My Mummy is a Mummy
And she's a doctor too.
When she's not looking after me,
She's looking after you!

John and Jim

I've got a secret friend
Who lives at home with me.
Even when we're talking
There's no one there to see.
> My name's John and his name's Jim.
> You can see me, but you can't see him.

I've got a secret friend
Who goes to school with me.
Even when we're walking
There's no one there to see.
> My name's John and his name's Jim.
> You can see me, but you can't see him.

I've got a secret friend
Who sits in class with me.
Even when we're writing
There's no one there to see.
> My name's John and his name's Jim.
> You can see me, but you can't see him.

I've got a secret friend
Who likes to box with me.
Even when we're fighting
There's no one there to see.
> My name's John and his name's Jim.
> You can see me, but you can't see him.

Dads

Monday, Tuesday, Wednesday,
Thursday and Friday too,
Daddies have to go to work,
And this is what they do:

Dads paint ships
And Dads fry chips!
Dads sell cars
And Dads fill jars!

Monday, Tuesday, Wednesday,
Thursday and Friday too,
Daddies have to go to work,
And this is what they do:

Dads fly planes
And Dads drive trains!
Dads build boats
And Dads make coats!

Monday, Tuesday, Wednesday,
Thursday and Friday too,
Daddies have to go to work,
And this is what they do:

Dads saw logs
And Dads feed hogs!
Dads write books
And Dads make hooks!

Monday, Tuesday, Wednesday,
Thursday and Friday too,
Daddies have to go to work,
And this is what they do:

Dads keep bees
And Dads sell cheese!
Dads make keys
And Dads fell trees!

Daddies have to go to work
And this is what they do.

What's in your hand?

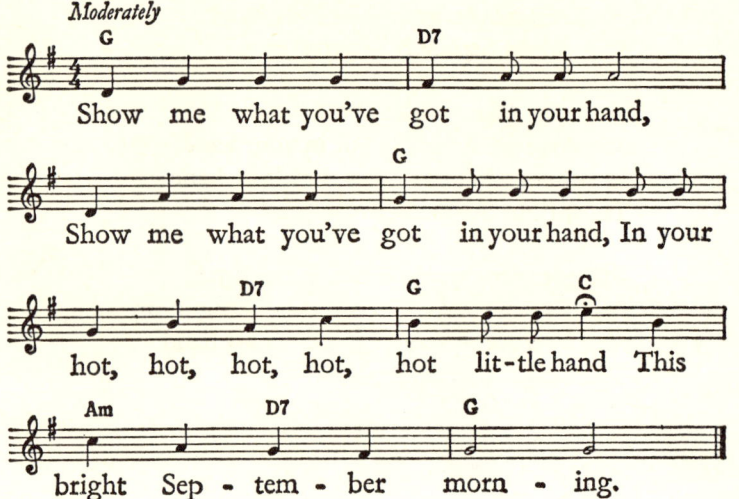

Show me what you've got in your hand,
Show me what you've got in your hand,
In your hot, hot, hot, hot, hot little hand
This bright September morning.

I've got a pink ice cream in my hand,
I've got a pink ice cream in my hand,
A pink ice cream in my hot little hand
This bright September morning.

Show me what you've got in your hand,
Show me what you've got in your hand,
In your hot, hot, hot, hot, hot little hand
This bright September morning.

I've got some Christmas pudding in my hand,
And I've got a pink ice cream in my hand,
Pudding and ice in my hot little hand
This bright September morning.

Show me what you've got in your hand,
Show me what you've got in your hand,
In your hot, hot, hot, hot, hot little hand
This bright September morning.

I've got some wobbly jelly in my hand,
And I've got some Christmas pudding in my hand,
And I've got a pink ice cream in my hand
This bright September morning.

Tip-toe

Tip-toe, tip-toe,
This is how I go
Through the house
Like a mouse.
No one can hear me.

Tip-toe, tip-toe,
Out into the soft snow.
Not a sound
All around –
No one comes near me.

Bye Baby Bunting

Bye Ba - by Bunt - ing, Dad - dy's gone a hunt - ing To fetch a lit - tle rab - bit skin To wrap the Ba - by Bunt-ing in. Bye Ba - by Bun -ting.

Bye Baby Bunting,
Daddy's gone a-hunting
To fetch a little rabbit skin
To wrap the Baby Bunting in.
Bye Baby Bunting.

My shoes were too small

My shoes were too small,
I couldn't get them on at all.

My coat was too long,
It touched the ground as I went along.

My hat was too wide,
My head got lost when it went inside.

What's inside?

What's inside my big brown basket?
There's a big jug of milk
And a small piece of silk.
That's what's inside my big brown basket.

What's inside my big brown bag?
There's a big piece of ham
And a small pot of jam.
That's what's inside my big brown bag.

What's inside my big brown box?
There's a big pot of stew
And a small tube of glue.
That's what's inside my big brown box.

Sing a song of work to do

Sing a song of work to do.
Mother has to make a stew,
Grandpa has to mend a dish,
Grandma has to cook some fish,
And I've been busy all day long
Writing down this little song.

Martin has to paint his boat,
Mary has to mend her coat,
Simon has to clean the shed,
Sally has to make her bed,
And I've been busy all day long
Writing down this little song.

Johnnie has to beat the mat,
Jennie has to feed the cat,
Mandy has to brush her hair,
Mother has to dust the chair,
And I've been busy all day long
Writing down this little song.

When I get dressed

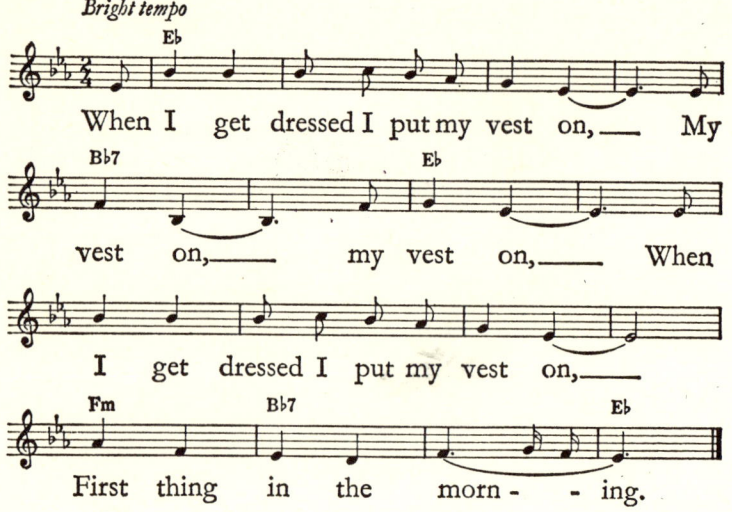

When I get dressed I put my vest on,
My vest on, my vest on,
When I get dressed I put my vest on,
First thing in the morning.

When I get dressed I put my pants on, *etc.*

When I get dressed I put my socks on, *etc.*

When I get dressed I put my shirt on, *etc.*

When I get dressed I put my trousers/skirt on, *etc.*

And when I'm dressed I eat my breakfast, *etc.*

Hushabye baby

Gently

Hush-a-bye ba - by, on the tree top,
When the wind blows the cra - dle will rock.
When the bough breaks the cra - dle will fall.
Down will come ba - by, cra - dle and all.

Hushabye baby, on the tree top,
When the wind blows the cradle will rock.
When the bough breaks the cradle will fall.
Down will come baby, cradle and all.

Clickety-click and clickety-clack

Five little ducks

Five little ducks swam out one day,
Over the pond and far away.
Mother Duck said 'Quack, quack, quack!'
And five little ducks came swimming back.

Four little ducks ...

Three little ducks ...

Two little ducks ...

One little duck ...

Aeroplanes, aeroplanes

Aeroplanes, aeroplanes, look where they fly.
Aeroplanes, aeroplanes, high in the sky.
Their engines are noisy; they make a loud hum.
Now I'm a plane. Look out! Here I come!

Clickety-click and clickety-clack

Clickety-click and clickety-clack,
The train goes rattling past.
Clickety-click and clickety-clack,
It's noisy and it's fast.

Clickety-click and clickety-clack,
It's going to the sea.
Clickety-click and clickety-clack,
One day it will take me.

Clickety-clack and clickety-click

Clickety-clack and clickety-click,
I'm on a train and it's going too quick.

Clickety-cloo and clickety-cloo,
I'm going to London to see the zoo.

Clickety-click and clickety-clack,
I'm on a train and I'm coming back.

Early in the morning

Early in the morning,
At the break of day,
The cockerel is the first to wake
And this is what he'll say:

Cock-a-doodle-doo!

Quietly

Hush, hush, hush,
Quiet as a mouse.
Hush, hush, hush,
All about the house.

Shhh, shhh, shhh.
Do not make a sound.
Shhh, shhh, shhh,
Creeping round and round.

Ring-a-ring-o'-roses

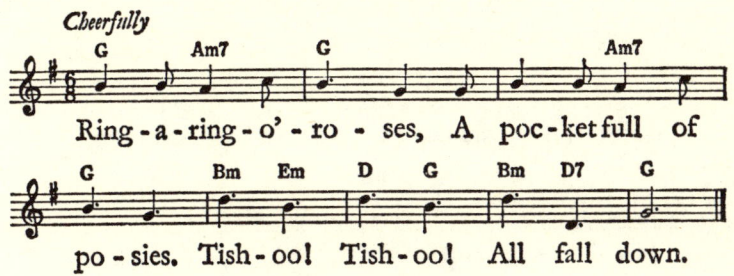

Ring-a-ring-o'-roses,
A pocket full of posies.
Tishoo! Tishoo!
All fall down.

Ten fat sausages

Ten fat sausages frying in the pan,
Ten fat sausages frying in the pan,
One went POP and another went BANG!
Then there were eight fat sausages frying in the pan.

Eight fat sausages frying in the pan,
Eight fat sausages frying in the pan,
One went POP and another went BANG!
Then there were six fat sausages frying in the pan.

Six fat sausages frying in the pan,
Six fat sausages frying in the pan,
One went POP and another went BANG!
Then there were four fat sausages frying in the pan.

Four fat sausages frying in the pan,
Four fat sausages frying in the pan,
One went POP and another went BANG!
Then there were two fat sausages frying in the pan.

Two fat sausages frying in the pan,
Two fat sausages frying in the pan,
One went POP and another went BANG!
Then there were no fat sausages frying in the pan!

Early in the morning

Come down to the station early in the morning,
See all the railway trains standing in a row.
See all the drivers starting up the engines,
Clickety click and clickety clack,
Off they go!

Come down to the garage early in the morning,
See all the buses standing in a row.
See all the drivers starting up the engines,
Rumble, rumble, rumble, rumble,
Off they go!

Come down to the seaside early in the morning,
See all the motor-boats floating in a row.
See all the drivers starting up the engines,
Splishing, splishing, sploshing, sploshing,
Off they go!

Come down to the airport early in the morning,
See all the aeroplanes standing in a row.
See all the pilots starting up the engines,
Whirring, whirring, whirring, whirring,
Off they go

I scream

I scream,
You scream,
We all scream
For ice cream.

The spinning-wheel

Spin-ning-wheel go round and round,
Soft-ly, soft-ly hum-ming. Make a shirt for
my old man; Win-ter days are com-ing.

Spinning-wheel go round and round,
Softly, softly humming.
Make a shirt for my old man;
Winter days are coming.

Make a suit for my old man ...

Make a scarf ...

Make a hat ...

All alone

I'm alone in the house
Except for the mouse
Whose hole is under the stair,
And the sounds that I hear
All fill me with fear
As I sit here in my chair.

There's no one there
But I hear the squeaking of a door.
There's no one there
But I hear a board creak in the floor.
There's no one there
But I hear someone turn a key.
There's no one there
But I hear someone calling me . . .

I'm alone in the house
Except for the mouse
Whose hole is under the stair,
And the sounds that I hear
All fill me with fear
As I sit here in my chair.

What a noisy house!

My sister in the garden is call, call, calling;
The baby in his pram is bawl, bawl, bawling.

The clock in the hall is ding, ding, dinging;
The postman at the door is ring, ring, ringing.

Mother with her saucepans is clang, clang, clanging;
And I, with my hammer, am bang, bang, banging.

Oh, what a noisy house!

At the door

The postman raps hard when he comes to the door,
To tell us we'd better run quick for a letter.

And the baker taps softly when he's at the door,
Just to say that he's there and he has cakes to spare.

But the milkman cries 'Milko!' and opens the door,
He leaves four from his crate and won't bother to wait.

Dring! Dring!

Dring! Dring!
Telephone.
Dring! Dring!
Telephone.
Dring! Dring!
No one home.
Dring! Dring!
No one home.
Dring! Dring!
All alone.
Dring! Dring!
All alone.
Dring! Dring!
Lonely phone.
Dring! Dring!
Lonely phone.
Dring! Dring!

Very quiet

If you can hear a spoon stirring,
               a clock ticking,
               a cat purring,
               a mouse scratching,
                   Then it's very, very quiet.

In the morning

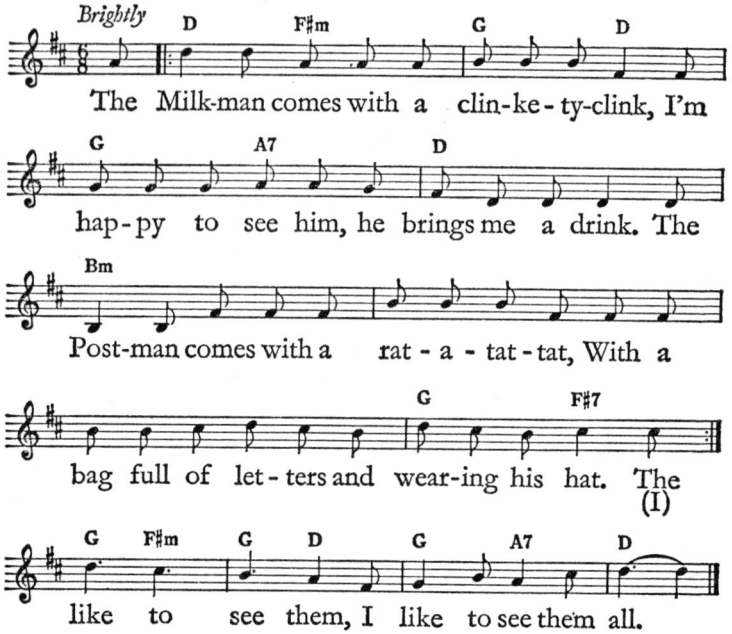

The Milkman comes with a clinkety-clink,
I'm happy to see him, he brings me a drink.
The Postman comes with a rat-a-tat-tat,
With a bag full of letters and wearing his hat.
The Dustman comes with a biffety-bang,
To take all our rubbish away in his van.
The paper boy comes with a 'Fiddle-de-dee,'
He always comes when I'm drinking my tea.
I like to see them,
I like to see them all.

Tooting and hooting

Tooting and hooting, tooting and hooting,
   That's how I drive my train each day.
I speed up the track and then I speed back,
   Hooting and tooting all the way.

Music

There's music in a hammer,
There's music in a nail,
There's music in a pussy cat
When you step on her tail!

Have you seen the boat leave?

Have you seen the boat leave?
It sails each day at three.
The engines whirr, the siren whines
And then it's off to sea.

Coming from the war

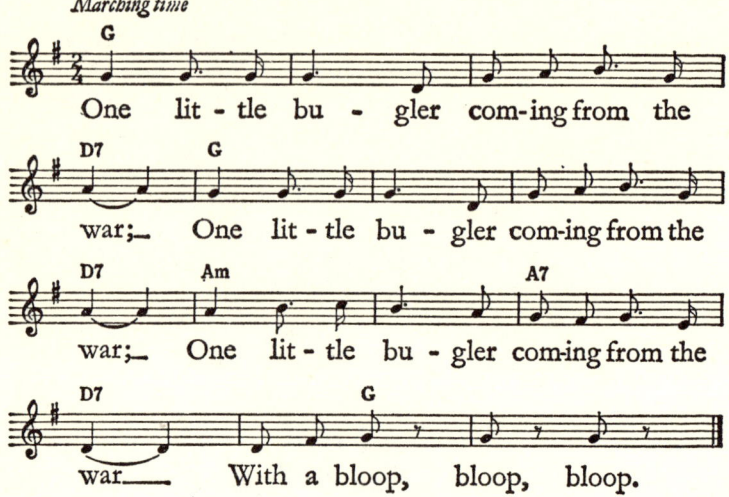

One little bugler coming from the war;
One little bugler coming from the war;
One little bugler coming from the war
With a bloop, bloop, bloop.

Two little pipers coming from the war;
Two little pipers coming from the war;
Two little pipers coming from the war
With a toot, toot, toot.

Three little drummers ...

Four little bandsmen ...

My little brother

I had a little brother
No bigger than my thumb;
I put him in the coffee pot –
He rattled like a drum!

TV

Bang! Bang! Bang!
The cowboys shoot.
Doo! Doo! Doo!
The trumpets toot.
Vroom! Vroom! Vroom!
The police cars roar.
'Turn it off!'
Dad slams the door.

Bought me a cat

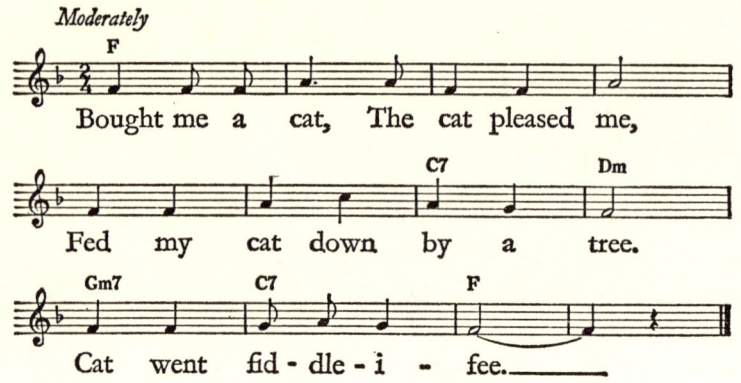

Bought me a cat,
The cat pleased me,
Fed my cat down by a tree.
Cat went fiddle-i-fee.

Bought me a hen,
The hen pleased me,
Fed my hen down by a tree.
Hen went chipsy, chipsy.

Bought me a duck,
The duck pleased me,
Fed my duck down by a tree.
Duck went slishy, sloshy.

Bought me a goose,
The goose pleased me,
Fed my goose down by a tree.
Goose went qua, qua, qua, qua.

Bought me a dog,
The dog pleased me,
Fed my dog down by a tree.
Dog went wow, wow, wow, wow.

Bought me a sheep,
The sheep pleased me,
Fed my sheep down by a tree.
Sheep went baa, baa, baa, baa.

Bought me a cow,
The cow pleased me,
Fed my cow down by a tree.
Cow went moo, moo, moo, moo.

Bought me a horse,
The horse pleased me,
Fed my horse down by a tree.
Horse went neigh, neigh, neigh, neigh.

Ride a cock horse

Ride a cock horse to Banbury Cross
To see a fine lady upon a white horse;
With rings on her fingers and bells on her toes,
She shall have music wherever she goes.

In the kitchen

The saucepan lids went clang
And the door blew shut with a bang,
The kitchen tap went shhshhshhshhshhh
And the whistling kettle sang.

The timer went off with a ping
And the doorbell began to ring,
The dog joined in with a woof, woof, woof,
And then Daddy began to sing!

Hello, hello, hello!

'Hello, hello, hello, sir,
Meet me at the grocer.'
'No, sir.'
'Why, sir?'
'Because I have a cold, sir.'
'Where did you get your cold, sir?'
'At the North Pole, sir.'
'What were you doing there, sir?'
'Shooting polar bear, sir.'
'Let me hear you sneeze, sir.'
'Atishoo, atishoo, atishoo, sir!'

The music man

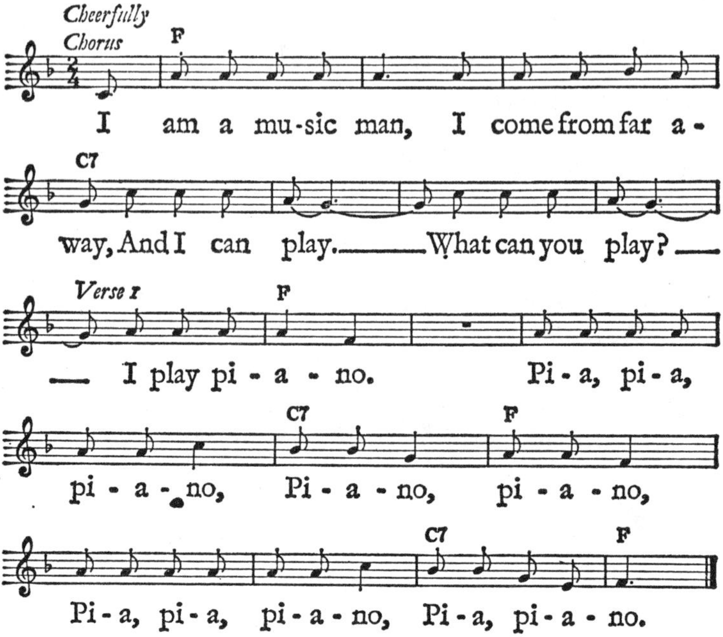
Cheerfully
Chorus
F
I am a mu-sic man, I come from far a-
C7
way, And I can play. What can you play?
Verse 1
F
I play pi - a - no. Pi - a, pi - a,
C7
F
pi - a - no, Pi - a - no, pi - a - no,
C7
F
Pi - a, pi - a, pi - a - no, Pi - a, pi - a - no.

Chorus *I am a music man,*
I come from far away,
And I can play.
What can you play?

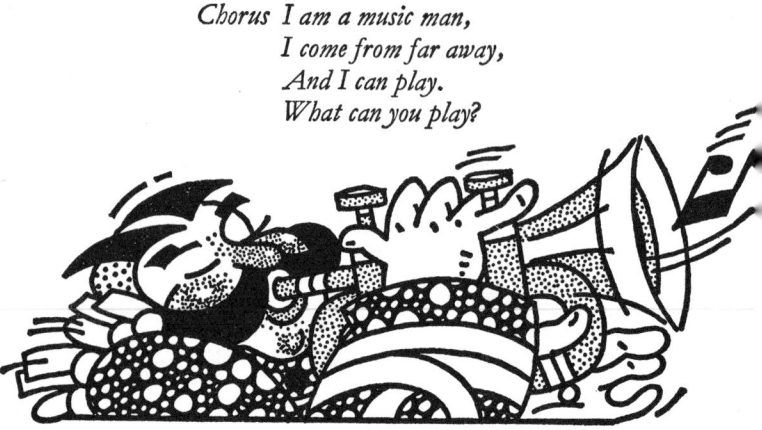

I play piano.
Pi-a, pi-a, pi-a-no,
Piano, piano,
Pi-a, pi-a, pi-a-no,
Pi-a, piano.

I play the big drum.
Boom-di, boom-di, boom-di-boom,
Boom-di-boom, boom-di-boom,
Boom-di, boom-di, boom-di-boom,
Boom-di, boom-di-boom.
Pi-a, pi-a, pi-a-no,
Piano, piano,
Pi-a, pi-a, pi-a-no,
Pi-a, piano.

I play the trumpet.
Toot-ti, toot-ti, toot-ti-toot,
Toot-ti-toot, toot-ti-toot,
Toot-ti, toot-ti, toot-ti-toot,
Toot-ti, toot-ti-toot.
Boom-di, boom-di, boom-di-boom, *etc.*
Pi-a, pi-a, pi-a-no, *etc.*

Bells are ringing

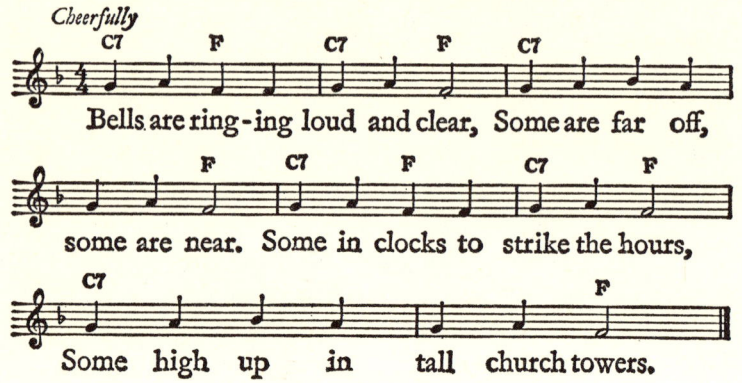

Bells are ringing loud and clear,
Some are far off, some are near.
Some in clocks to strike the hours,
Some high up in tall church towers.

A little talk

The big brown hen and Mrs Duck
Went walking out together;
They talked about all sorts of things –
The farmyard and the weather.
But all I heard was: 'Cluck! Cluck! Cluck!'
And 'Quack! Quack! Quack!' from Mrs Duck.

Noise

I like noise.
The huffing
the puffing
and buffing of a train.

The teeming
and splashing
and streaming of the rain.

The clashing
and bashing
and smashing of the plates.

The making
and baking
and scoffing of the cakes.

Bird song

Pigeon Don't scold so, Susie.
Don't scold so, Susie.
Don't scold so, Susie.
Don't.

Thrush Pretty Dick, pretty Dick, pretty Dick.
Come here! Come here! Come here!
Dear! Dear! Dear!

Cuckoo Cuckoo, Cuckoo,
Pray what do you do?
In April, I open my bill.
In May, I sing night and day.
In June, I change my tune.
In July, away I fly.
In August, away I must.

Cuckoo, Cuckoo,
Pray where do you go?
Up high, into the sky,
Far away over the sea,
To Spain, I fly again;
Day and night I take my flight.
Cuckoo,
Goodbye to you.

The band

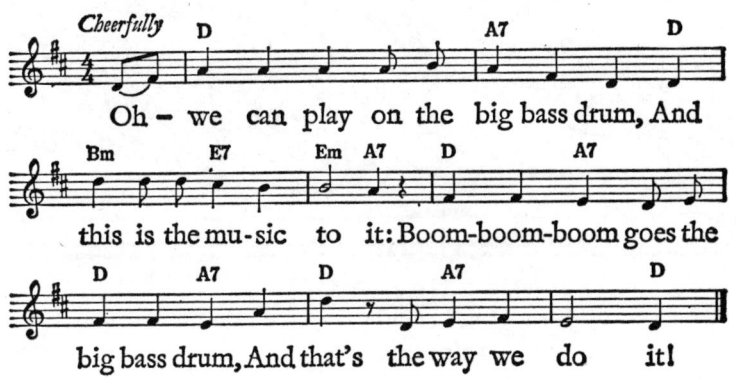

Oh – we can play on the big bass drum,
And this is the music to it:
Boom-boom-boom goes the big bass drum,
And that's the way we do it!

Oh – we can play on the violin,
And this is the music to it:
Zing-zing-zing goes the violin,
And that's the way we do it!

Oh – we can play on the saxophone,
And this is the music to it:
Soo-soo-soo goes the saxophone,
And that's the way we do it!

Oh – we can play on the tambourine,
And this is the music to it:
Tink-tink-tink goes the tambourine,
And that's the way we do it!

Jingle bells

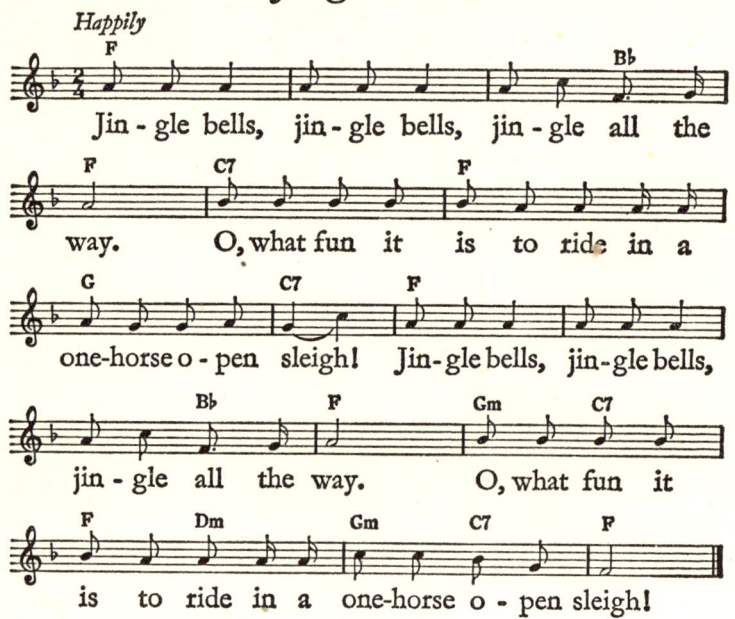

Jingle bells, jingle bells, jingle all the way.
O, what fun it is to ride in a one-horse open sleigh!
Jingle bells, jingle bells, jingle all the way.
O, what fun it is to ride in a one-horse open sleigh!

One little cockerel

One lit-tle cock-er-el bright and gay
Stood on a gate at break of day.
'Ho, lit-tle cock-er-el, how do you do?'
'Quite well, thank you. Cock-a-doo-dle-doo!'

One little cockerel bright and gay
Stood on a gate at break of day.
'Ho, little cockerel, how do you do?'
'Quite well, thank you. Cock-a-doodle-doo!'

Two little ponies dappled grey
Stood near a gate at break of day.
'Ho, little ponies, what do you say?'
'It's a lovely morning. Neigh! Neigh! Neigh!'

Three little puppies down our way
Played near a gate at break of day.
'Ho, little puppies, what is it now?'
'Please come and play too. Bow-wow-wow-wow!'

Oranges and lemons

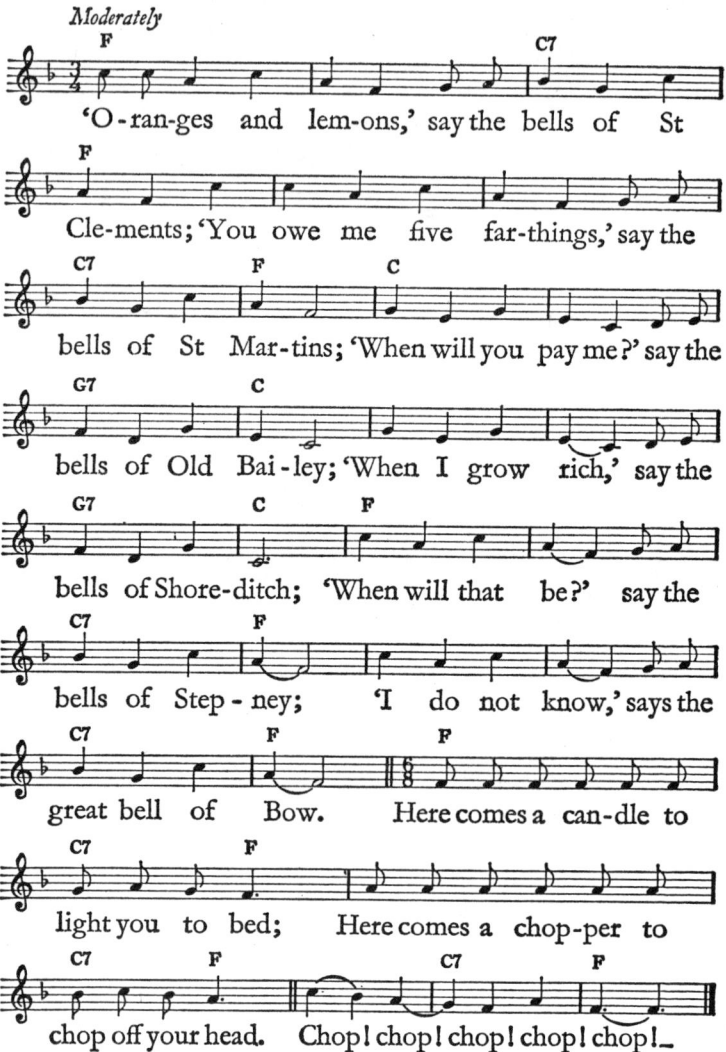

'Oranges and lemons,' say the bells of St Clements;
'You owe me five farthings,' say the bells of St Martins;
'When will you pay me?' say the bells of Old Bailey;
'When I grow rich,' say the bells of Shoreditch;
'When will that be?' say the bells of Stepney;
'I do not know,' says the great bell of Bow.

Here comes a candle to light you to bed;
Here comes a chopper to chop off your head.
Chop! chop! chop! chop! chop!

Crash, bang!

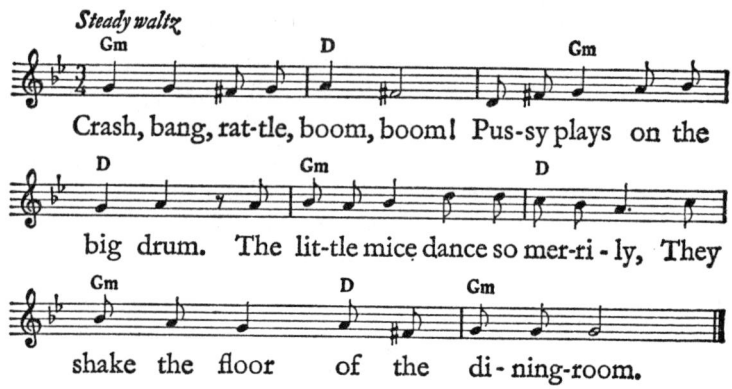

Crash, bang, rattle, boom, boom!
Pussy plays on the big drum.
The little mice dance so merrily,
They shake the floor of the dining-room.

I see Pussy sitting
On the roof with her kittens.
'It's freezing cold on the roof-top here,
So where shall we go for mittens?'

'Let's go off to Denmark,
Buy some mittens and run back.
And then we'll all dance together,
And care no more for the weather.'

I walked across the farmyard

I walked across the farmyard
And what did I see?
A big brown horse
Stood neighing at me.
Neigh, neigh, neigh, neigh, neigh!

I walked across the farmyard
And what did I see?
A big black cow
Stood mooing at me.
Moo, moo, moo, moo, moo!

I walked across the farmyard
And what did I see?
A big pink pig
Stood grunting at me.
Grunt, grunt, grunt, grunt, grunt!

This old man

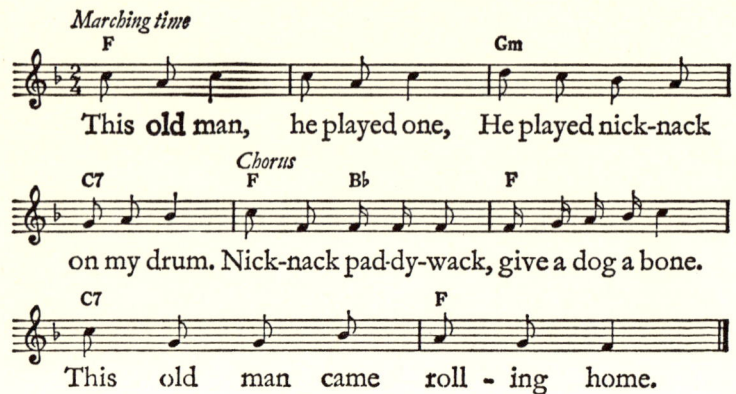

This old man, he played one,
He played nick-nack on my drum.

Chorus *Nick-nack paddy-wack, give a dog a bone.*
This old man came rolling home.

This old man, he played two,
He played nick-nack on my shoe.

This old man, he played three,
He played nick-nack on my knee.

This old man, he played four,
He played nick-nack on my door.

This old man, he played five,
He played nick-nack on my hive.

This old man, he played six,
He played nick-nack on my sticks.

This old man, he played seven,
He played nick-nack up in heaven.

This old man, he played eight,
He played nick-nack on my gate.

This old man, he played nine,
He played nick-nack on my spine.

This old man, he played ten,
He played nick-nack once again.

Who's there?

Rap, rap, rap went the window-cleaning man.
May I have some water?
Please put it in this can.

Clink, clink, clink, it's the milkman at the gate.
Do you want some milk today?
I'm sorry I am late.

Knock, knock, knock goes the postman at the door.
I've got a parcel here for you.
It's come from Singapore.

Bang, bang, bang, it's Johnny from the shop.
These are the things you wanted.
I've put the eggs on top.

Wibbleton to Wobbleton

Wibbleton to Wobbleton

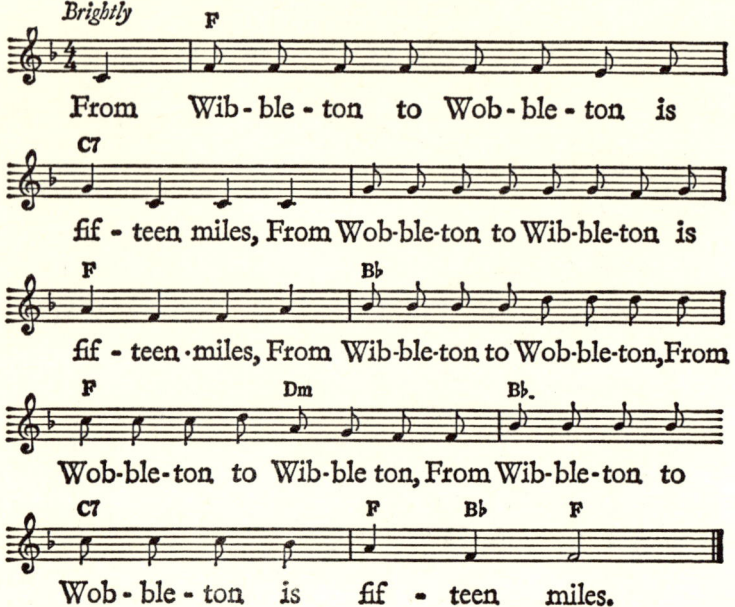

From Wibbleton to Wobbleton is fifteen miles,
From Wobbleton to Wibbleton is fifteen miles,
From Wibbleton to Wobbleton,
From Wobbleton to Wibbleton,
From Wibbleton to Wobbleton is fifteen miles.

To market, to market

To mar-ket, to mar-ket, to buy a fat pig;
Home a-gain, home a-gain, jig-ge-ty jig. To
mar-ket, to mar-ket, to buy a fat hog;
Home a-gain, home a-gain, jig-ge-ty jog.

To market, to market, to buy a fat pig;
Home again, home again, jiggety jig.
To market, to market to buy a fat hog;
Home again, home again, jiggety jog.

My red balloon

This red balloon that I've got in my hand
Will take me away to a far-off land.

Chorus '*I've got a red balloon and can fly across the sea.*
You should get one too and then come along with me.'

Although it looks tiny, I've only to blow
To make it grow bigger, and grow and grow . . .

Until it will lift me into the sky,
Then over the trees and off I'll fly.

The people below will all stand and stare
When they see me floating by in the air.

So I'll wave to them as I drift along,
I'll wave my hand and I'll sing this song:

On a train

You can go to sleep on a train,
You can go to sleep on a train,
Just eat up your supper and get into bed,
Pull up the covers and put down your head.

Then in the morning you get up again
When you go to sleep on a train.

Come on board

One is one and two is two,
I'm a spaceman. Who are you?

Three is three and four is four,
Listen to my spaceship's roar.

Five is five and six is six,
Come on board, we must be quick.

Seven is seven, eight is eight,
Wouldn't you like to be my mate?

Nine is nine and ten is ten,
You will not see earth again.

Bobby Shafto

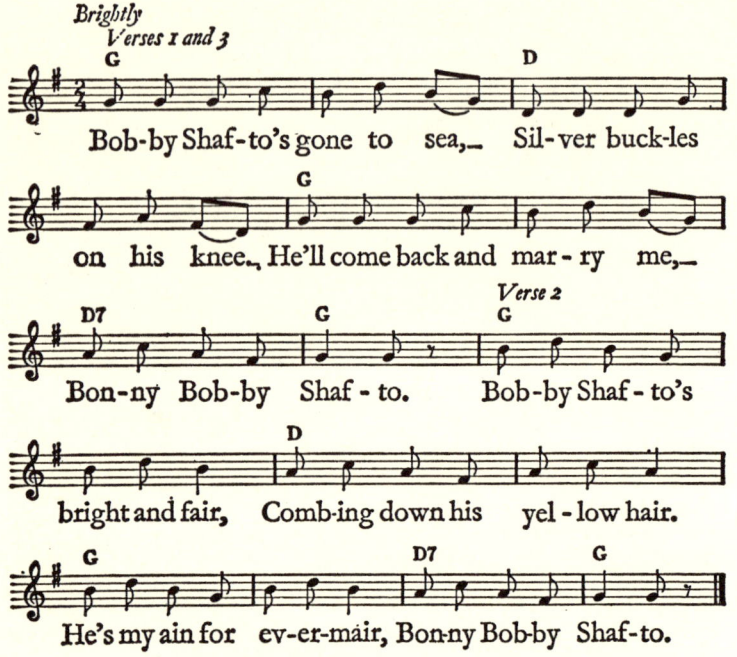

Bobby Shafto's gone to sea,
Silver buckles on his knee.
He'll come back and marry me,
Bonny Bobby Shafto.

Bobby Shafto's bright and fair,
Combing down his yellow hair.
He's may ain (*own*) for ever-mair,
Bonny Bobby Shafto.

Bobby Shafto's been to sea,
Silver buckles on his knee.
He's come back and married me,
Bonny Bobby Shafto.

Sing a song of spaceships

Sing a song of spaceships
Glinting in the sky;
I run indoors and lock the door
When they come swooping by.
Sing a song of spaceships;
I never stay to see
The men who come to earth from space –
They may be after me!

Ten galloping horses

Ten galloping horses came to town,
Five were white, and five were brown.
They galloped up, they galloped down,
And then they galloped right out of town.

Rocket song

Boom off!
Zoom off!
Now we're on our way.
Our rocket's left the launching pad
And we're in space today.

Drop down!
Plop down!
Get the buggy out.
It's just the thing upon the moon
To help us get about.

Crash down!
Splash down!
We go back to a ship
With cheers and claps and handshakes
To end our first moon trip.

Willy boy, where are you going?

Willy boy, Willy boy, where are you going?
  I will go with you, if I may –
I am going to the meadows to see them mowing,
  I am going to see them make the hay.

Johnny boy, Johnny boy, where are you going?
  I will go with you, if you please –
I am going to the dairy to watch them working,
  I am going to see them make the cheese.

Dicky boy, Dicky boy, where are you going?
  I will go with you, if you wish –
I am going to the harbour to watch them landing,
  I am going to see them bring in fish.

The big ship sails

The big ship sails through the al-ly, al-ly O, The al-ly, al-ly O, the al-ly, al-ly O, The big ship sails through the al-ly, al-ly O, On the last day of De-cem-ber.

The big ship sails through the ally, ally O,
The ally, ally O, the ally, ally O,
The big ship sails through the ally, ally O,
On the last day of December.

Three boats

I saw three boats come sailing by,
Sailing by, sailing by;
I waved as each boat came sailing by
And hoped they'd be friends with me.

The first was a liner with funnels and steam,
Funnels and steam, funnels and steam;
But he went on puffing and just didn't seem
To want to be friends with me.

The next was a yacht with a sail and a mast,
Sail and a mast, sail and a mast;
But he took no notice and just glided past
And wouldn't be friends with me.

The third was a tugboat so tiny and slow,
Tiny and slow, tiny and slow;
But he blew his hooter and shouted 'Hello!'
And he was a friend to me.

Pussy-cat

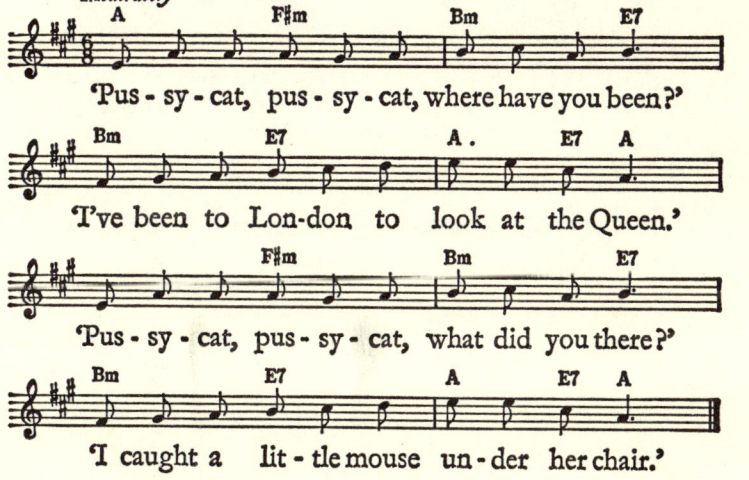

'Pus - sy - cat, pus - sy - cat, where have you been?'
'I've been to Lon-don to look at the Queen.'
'Pus - sy - cat, pus - sy - cat, what did you there?'
'I caught a lit - tle mouse un - der her chair.'

'Pussy-cat, pussy-cat, where have you been?'
'I've been to London to look at the Queen.'
'Pussy-cat, pussy-cat, what did you there?'
'I caught a little mouse under her chair.'

Sitting on a pony

Lazily

Sit-ing on a po-ny, rid-ing in-to town,
Jogg-ing down the road, bobb-ing up and down;
Gee up Ned-dy,— please don't stop,
Clipp-e-ty, clipp-e-ty, clipp-e-ty, clop.

Sitting on a pony, riding into town,
Jogging down the road, bobbing up and down;
Gee up Neddy, please don't stop,
Clippety, clippety, clippety, clop.

Going up the hill

Going up the hill
The horse is very slow,
The hill is very steep,
There's a long way to go.
But coming down he goes ...
Ever so fast.

Going up the hill
He finds it very rough,
The horse is very tired,
He's nearly had enough.
But coming down he goes ...
Ever so fast.

Going up the hill
He's just about to stop,
The horse will have a job
To make it to the top.
But coming down he goes ...
Ever so fast.

The buses and the motor cars

The buses and the motor cars
Go round the city square;
Up the hill, round the corner,
And all the way up there.

Quicker by bike

I like to hike –
But it's quicker by bike!

Catch a whale

Let's go to the seaside
And take a great big pail.
We can dip it in the water
And we might catch a whale!

The wheels on the bus

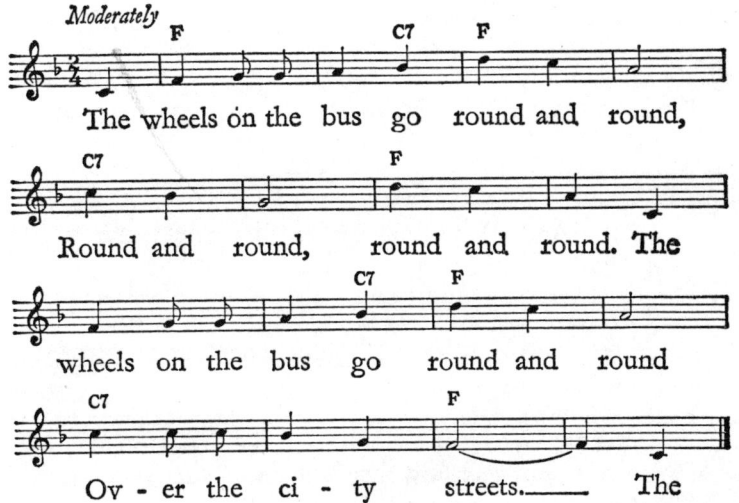

The wheels on the bus go round and round,
Round and round, round and round.
The wheels on the bus go round and round
Over the city streets.

The horn on the bus goes peep, peep, peep, *etc.*

The mums on the bus go chatter, chatter, chatter, *etc.*

The dads on the bus go nod, nod, nod, *etc.*

The kids on the bus go wriggle, wriggle, wriggle, *etc.*

The ride to London Town

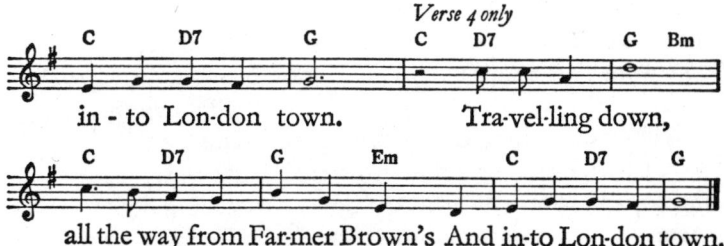

all the way from Far-mer Brown's And in-to Lon-don town.

*Repeat these two bars in verses 2-4 as often as necessary.

There were four jolly country men who worked for Farmer Brown,
And they decided they would take a ride to London town;
But one thing they weren't sure about was how they would get there.
'I know,' said the first, 'I'll take a ride on the back of the old grey mare.'
So he jumped on the back of the old grey mare and he jogged off down the road.
Clip clop clip clop clip went the horse – travelling down,
All the way from Farmer Brown's and into London town.

But the second man was not so sure that this was the way to go.
'It's not much good if it rains,' he said, 'and a horse is much too slow;
If ever I want to go for a ride, the way I like best by far
Is sitting on a seat behind the steering-wheel of a motor car,'
So he opened the door and he jumped inside and he drove off down the road.
Brrrm brrrm brrrm brrrm brrrm went the car and
Clip clop clip clop clip went the horse – travelling down,
All the way from Farmer Brown's and into London town.

But then it was the third man's turn, and this is what he said:
'A car runs out of petrol, and a horse, it must be fed.
The road is far too bumpy and it's twisting all the while;
I'd rather catch a railway train and travel there in style.'
So he went to the station and jumped on board and chugged
off down the line.
Chug chug chug chug chug went the train and
Brrrm brrrm brrrm brrrm brrrm went the car and
Clip clop clip clop clip went the horse – travelling down,
All the way from Farmer Brown's and into London town.

There was one on a horse and one in a car and one more on a
train,
But the last one thought he'd rather go for a ride in an
aeroplane;
'The thing that I like best,' he said, 'is zooming through the
sky;
If ever I want to go somewhere I always like to fly.'
So he bought his ticket and jumped on a plane and he sailed
off through the sky.
Zoom zoom zoom went the plane and
Chug chug chug chug chug went the train and
Brrrm brrrm brrrm brrrm brrrm went the car and
Clip clop clip clop clip went the horse – travelling down,
All the way from Farmer Brown's and into London town.
Travelling down, all the way from Farmer Brown's
And into London town.

Round and round the village

Clap hands

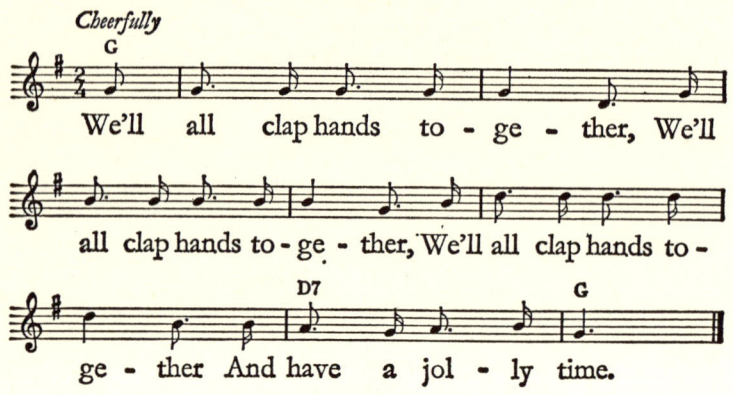

We'll all clap hands together,
We'll all clap hands together,
We'll all clap hands together
And have a jolly time.

... stamp feet ...

... wave arms ...

... march round ...

... nod heads ...

... hop round ...

Round and round the village

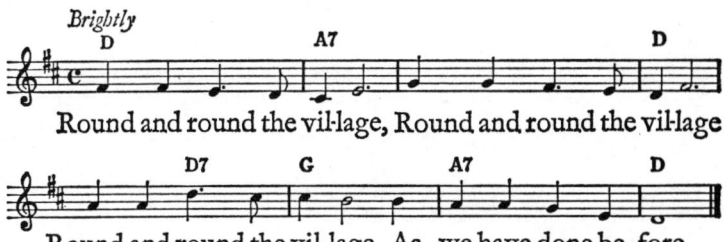

Round and round the vil-lage, Round and round the vil-lage
Round and round the vil-lage, As we have done be-fore.

Round and round the village,
Round and round the village,
Round and round the village
As we have done before.

In and out the windows,
In and out the windows,
In and out the windows
As we have done before.

Stand and face your playmate ...

Follow him to London ...

Lead him round the houses ...

Bow before you leave him ...

If you take a piece of wood

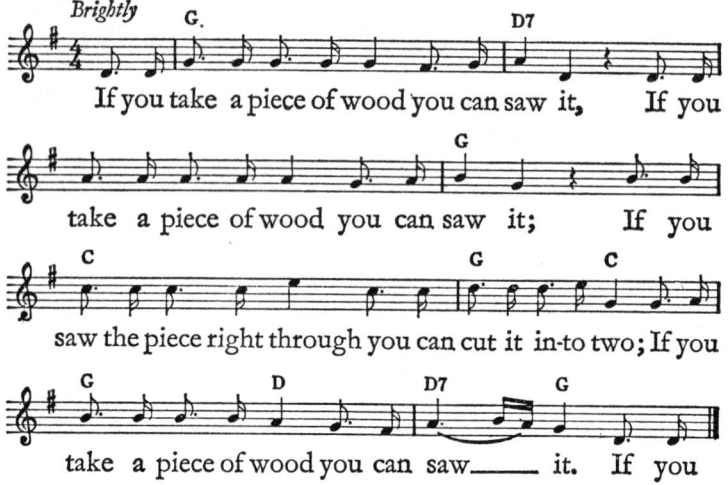

If you take a piece of wood you can saw it,
If you take a piece of wood you can saw it;
If you saw the piece right through you can cut it into two;
If you take a piece of wood you can saw it.

If you take a piece of wood you can drill it,
If you take a piece of wood you can drill it;
And like a little mole you can make yourself a hole;
If you take a piece of wood you can drill it.

If you take a piece of wood you can nail it,
If you take a piece of wood you can nail it;
You've only got to stand with a hammer in your hand;
If you take a piece of wood you can nail it.

If you take a piece of wood you can chop it,
If you take a piece of wood you can chop it;
You'll find it quickly splits into lots of little bits;
If you take a piece of wood you can chop it.

A little rabbit

A little rabbit on a hill
Was bobbing up and down;
His tail was soft and white,
His two long ears were brown.
But when he heard a roaring noise
Made by the farmer's van,
His tiny whiskers trembled
And down his hole he ran.

Five little kittens

Five little kittens crept out one day,
Over the fields and far away.
Mother cat said 'Mew, mew, mew.
Those naughty kittens! What shall I do?'

The Christmas pudding

Into the basin put the plums,
Stir-about, stir-about, stir-about!

Next the good white flour comes,
Stir-about, stir-about, stir-about!

Sugar and peel and eggs and spice,
Stir-about, stir-about, stir-about!

Mix them and fix them and cook them twice,
Stir-about, stir-about, stir-about!

Five little ladies

Five little ladies sitting in a row,
Five little gentlemen bow down low.
Five little ladies get up and walk away.
Five little gentlemen go off alone to play.

Smoke goes up the chimney

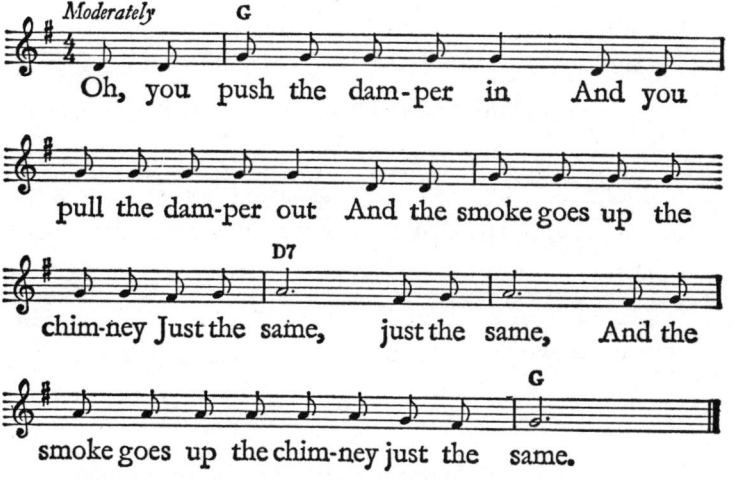

Oh, you push the damper in
And you pull the damper out
And the smoke goes up the chimney
Just the same, just the same,
And the smoke goes up the chimney just the same.

See-saw, Margery Daw

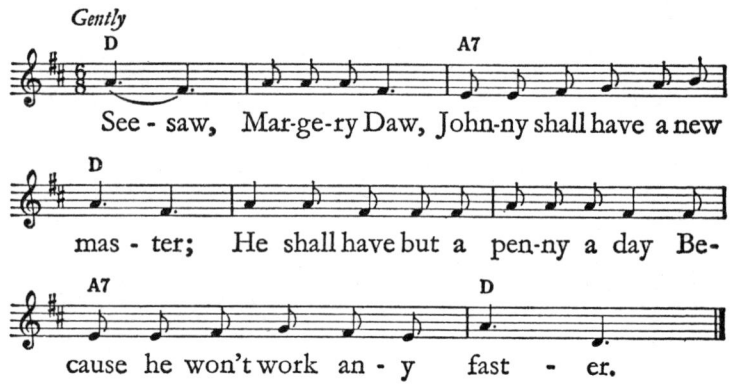

See-saw, Margery Daw,
   Johnny shall have a new master;
  He shall have but a penny a day
    Because he won't work any faster.

See-saw, sacaradown,
   Which is the way to London town?
  One foot up, and the other foot down,
    That is the way to London town!

Put out your arm

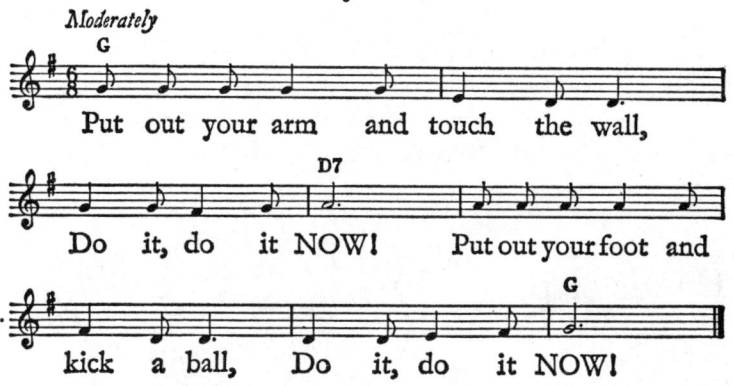

Put out your arm and touch the wall,
Do it, do it NOW!
Put out your foot and kick a ball,
Do it, do it NOW!

Put out your hand and touch your nose,
Do it, do it NOW!
Bend your knees and feel your toes,
Do it, do it NOW!

Climb a ladder to the top,
Do it, do it NOW!
Around the room on one leg hop,
Do it, do it NOW!

Now you sit down on the floor,
Do it, do it NOW!
No one moves, not any more,
Do it, do it NOW!

Two clean hands

Two clean hands and two fat thumbs,
Eight little fingers, ten little toes,
One round head goes nod, nod, nodding,
Two eyes peeping, one tiny nose.

Hands clap

Hands clap,
Fingers wriggle,
Arms wave,
Thumbs wiggle.
Toes waggle,
Heels thump,
Legs run,
Feet jump.

Five fingers

Five fingers wriggling, wriggling,
Now they stand still.
Four fingers waggling, waggling,
Now they stand still.
Three fingers moving, moving,
Now they stand still,
Two fingers bending, bending,
Now they stand still.
One thumb wiggling, wiggling,
Now it stands still.

The water snake

Down among the lilies, over in the lake
Pretending he's asleep, there lies a water snake.
When he hears the grasses blow
He moves his body to and fro,
Up and down and round about,
See him slowly coming out!
Now his jaws are open wide –
My poor finger is inside!

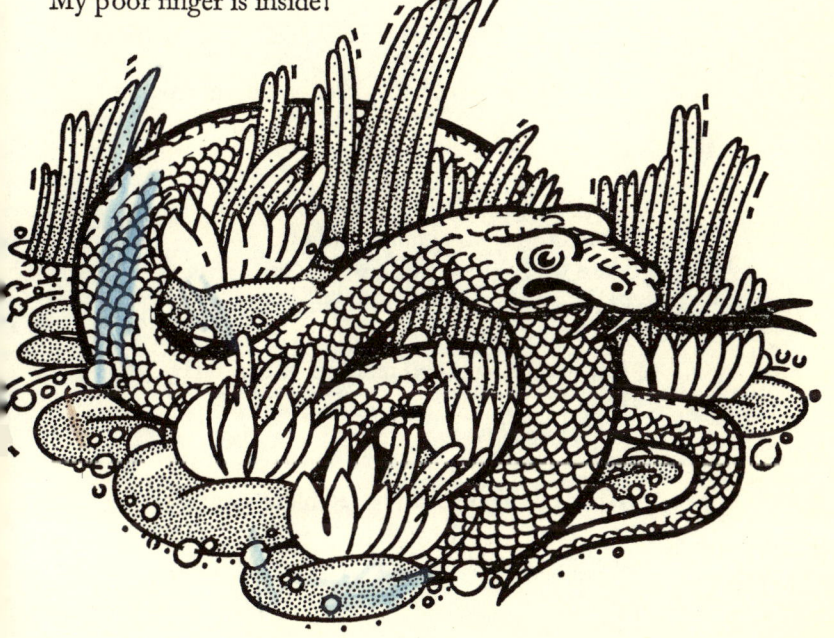

Knock, knock

Knock, knock at the door,
Pull, pull down the bell,
Peep, peep through the keyhole,
Turn, turn the handle
And walk right in.

Here we come gathering nuts in May

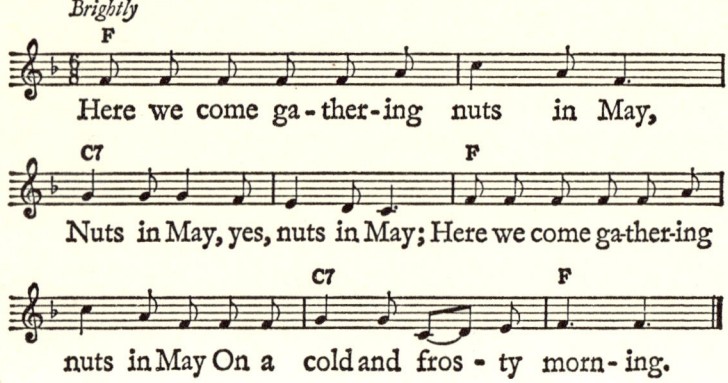

Here we come gathering nuts in May,
Nuts in May, yes, nuts in May;
Here we come gathering nuts in May
On a cold and frosty morning.

And whom will you take for nuts in May?

We'll take *Jane Brown* for nuts in May.

Whom will you send to fetch her away?

We'll send *Martin Smith* to fetch her away.

Huntsman got up very early

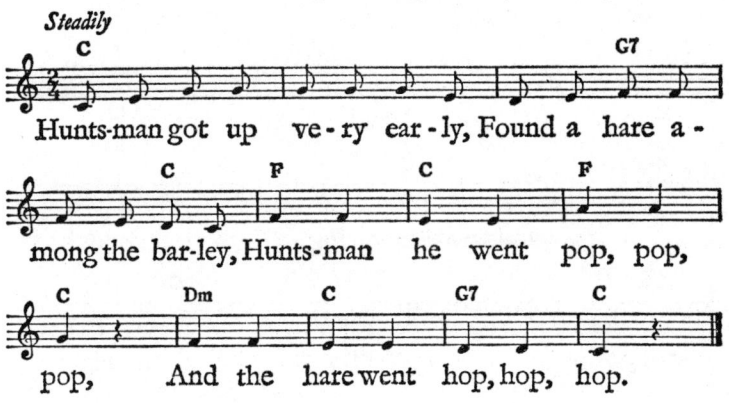

Huntsman got up very early,
Found a hare among the barley,
Huntsman he went pop, pop, pop,
And the hare went hop, hop, hop.

Huntsman spies him in the bushes,
After him with gun he rushes,
Huntsman he goes pop, pop, pop,
But the hare goes hop, hop, hop.

Jumping Jack

Jack be nimble,
Jack be quick,
Jack jump over the candlestick.

Hands are cold

Hands are cold and feet are cold;
Icy winds are blowing.
Rub your hands and stamp your feet
And soon they will be glowing.

Planting beans

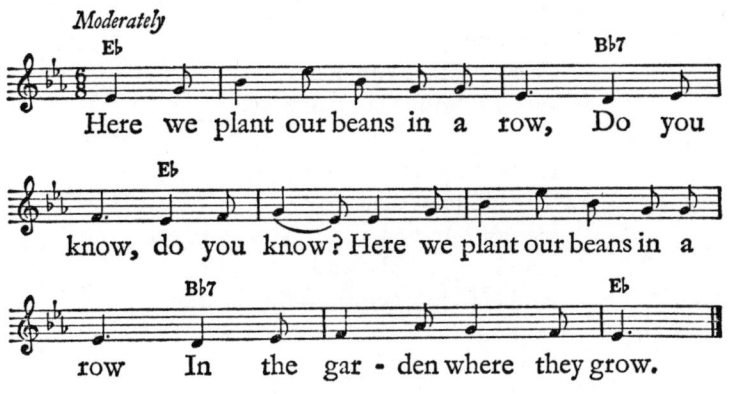

Here we plant our beans in a row,
Do you know, do you know?
Here we plant our beans in a row
In the garden where they grow.

With our toe we plant them so,
Do you know, do you know?
With our toe we plant them so
In the garden where they grow.

With our foot we plant them so . . .

With our heel we plant them so . . .

With our fist we plant them so . . .

With our nose we plant them so . . .

Rain, rain, go away

Rain, rain, go away,
Come again another day,
Little Johnny wants to play.

It's raining, it's pouring,
The old man's snoring;
He got into bed
And bumped his head
And couldn't get up in the morning.

Rain, rain, go to Spain
And never show your face again.

Smell a rose

Smell a rose
With your nose.
Put this fish
On a dish.
Chase the cat
Off the mat.
Wave your hand
To the band.

Clap your hands

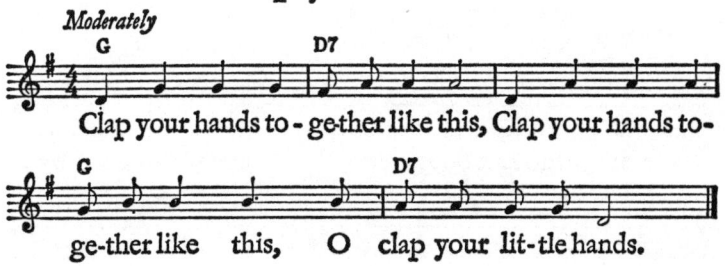

Clap your hands together like this,
Clap your hands together like this,
O clap your little hands.

Clap your feet together like this . . .

Clap your knees together like this . . .

Clap your heels together like this . . .

Looby Loo

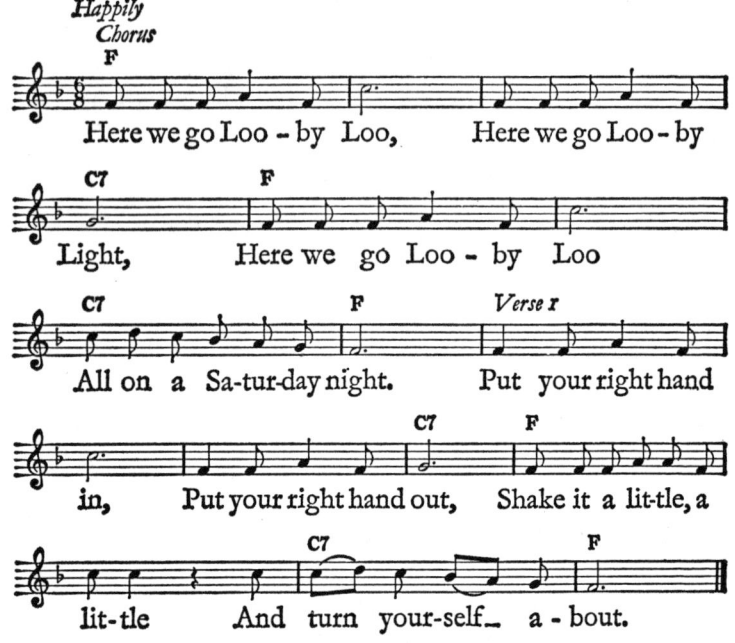

Chorus *Here we go Looby Loo,*
Here we go Looby Light,
Here we go Looby Loo
All on a Saturday night.

Put your right hand in,
Put your right hand out,
Shake it a little, a little
And turn yourself about.

Put your left hand in ...

Put your right foot in ...

Put your left foot in ...

Put your right hip in ...

Put your left hip in ...

Put your big nose in ...

Put your whole self in ...

There was a little dog

There was a little dog sitting by the fireside;
Out popped a little coal,
And in the little doggie's tail
It burnt a little hole.
Away ran the little dog, to seek a little pool
To cool his little tail,
And for want of a better place,
He popped it in the pail,
He popped it in the pail,
And wiggle waggle, wiggle waggle,
Wiggle waggle, wiggle waggle
Went the doggie's tail.

Foxy's running

Foxy's running with a sack Full of ginger on his back. Chase him, rabbit, up the road; Try to make him drop his load.

Foxy's running with a sack
Full of ginger on his back.
Chase him, rabbit, up the road;
Try to make him drop his load.

Foxy's running with a sack
Full of ginger on his back.
Hurry, hedgehog, to the top;
With your prickles make him stop.

Hop a little

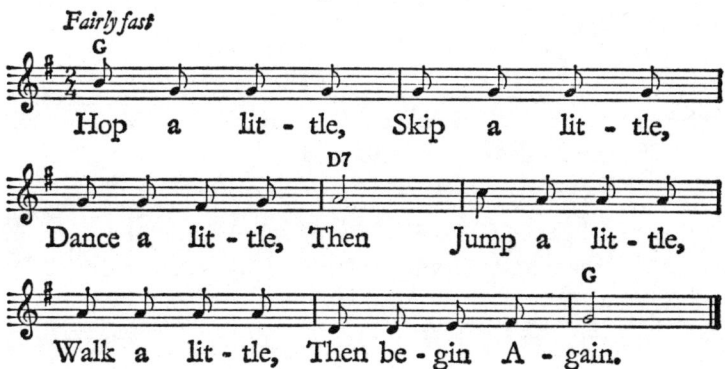

Hop a little,
Skip a little,
Dance a little,
Then

Jump a little,
Walk a little,
Then begin
Again.

Hop a little,
Skip a little,
Dance a little,
Then

Jump a little,
Walk a little,
Then begin
Again.

Up and down

Up and down, high and low,
Hands on head, hands on toe;
Up and down, high and low,
Hands on head, hands on toe;
Come and join us – have a go.

On the see-saw, high and low,
Down you come, up I go;
I go up, you come down,
You go up, I come down;
When you're up, I'm on the ground.

On the swings, high and low,
Down you come, up you go;
Swinging high, swinging low,
Down you come, up you go;
On the swings – have a go.

Up and down, that's the game,
Rest and play, just the same;
Up to bed – I've started yawning,   ⎫
But I'll be down again in the morning. ⎬ *slowly*

Up and down, high and low,
Hands on head, hands on toe,
Up and down, high and low,
Hands on head, hands on toe,
Come and join us – have a go.

Pedal fast

Push with your feet and pedal fast
And sing this song with me:
'The thing I like is to ride my bike
As fast as fast can be.'

Going fishing

Did you ever go fishing on a bright sunny day –
Sit on a fence and have the fence give way?
Slide off the fence and rip your pants,
And see the little fishes do the hootchy-kootchy dance?

Jelly in the bowl

Jelly in the bowl,
Jelly in the bowl,
Wiggle waggle, wiggle waggle,
Jelly in the bowl.

Mousie in the hole,
Mousie in the hole,
Scritchy scratchy, scritchy scratchy,
Mousie in the hole.

Through the teeth

Through the teeth,
Past the gums,
Look out, stomach,
Here it comes!

Susie Simpkin went to France

Susie Simpkin went to France
To teach the ladies how to dance.
Tap your heel, then tap your toe,
All join hands and around we go.
Curtsy to the general,
Salute the captain,
Turn right round and start again.

Handy-Spandy, Jack-a-Dandy

Handy-Spandy, Jack-a-Dandy
Loves plum cake and sugar candy.
He bought some at the grocer's shop
And, pleased, away went hop, hop, hop!

Five trees

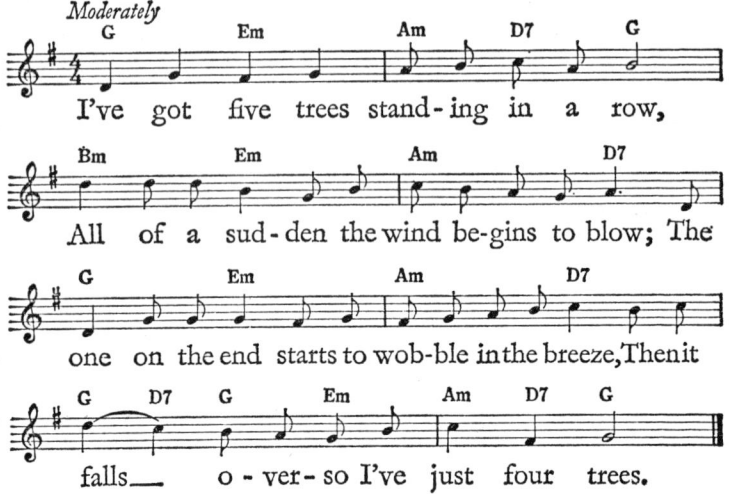

I've got five trees standing in a row,
All of a sudden the wind begins to blow;
The one on the end starts to wobble in the breeze,
Then it falls over – so I've just four trees.

I've got four trees standing in a row,
All of a sudden the wind begins to blow;
The next one along starts to wobble in the breeze,
Then it falls over – so I've just three trees.

I've got three trees ...

I've got two trees ...

Just one tree, standing all alone,
The wind comes along again and blows him on his own;
He shakes, and he bends, and he wobbles in the breeze,
And then he falls over – so I've no more trees.

I walked to the top of the hill

I walked to the top of the hill,
I walked to the top of the hill;
It began to rain,
So I came down again,
And I think it's raining still.

I ran to the grocer's shop,
I ran to the grocer's shop;
But the shop was full,
So I went to school
Without my lollipop.

I went to fly my plane,
I went to fly my plane;
It flew up in the air,
But I don't know where,
And it never came back again.

Dance to your Daddy

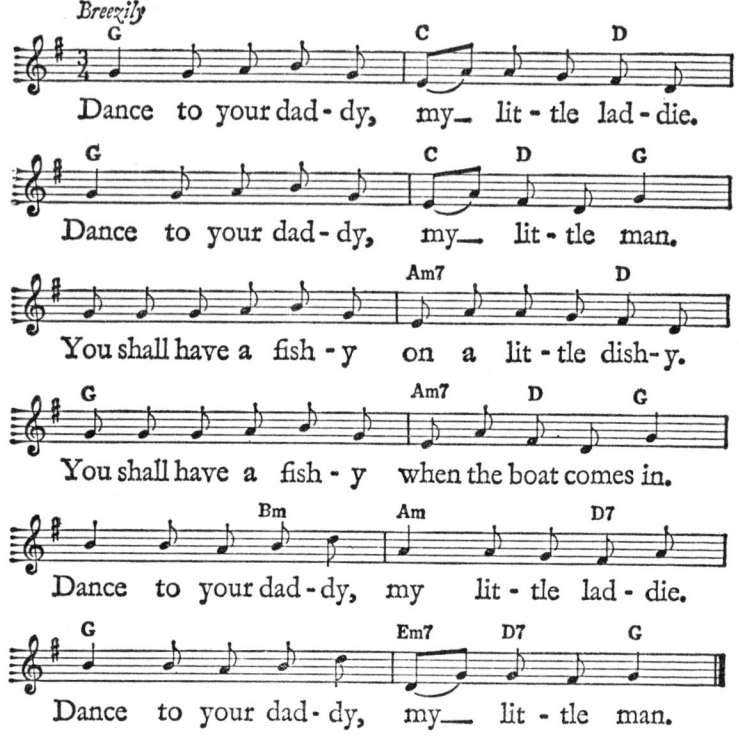

Dance to your daddy, my little laddie.
Dance to your daddy, my little man.
You shall have a fishy on a little dishy.
You shall have a fishy when the boat comes in.
Dance to your daddy, my little laddie.
Dance to your daddy, my little man.

If you want to do as I do

If you want to do as I do, clap your hands,
Clap your hands, clap your hands.
If you want to do as I do, clap your hands,
Clap your hands with me.

If you want to do as I do, nod your head,
Nod your head, nod your head.
If you want to do as I do, nod your head,
Nod your head with me.

... stamp your feet ...

... give a little whistle ...

... wave your hand ...

... wriggle your toes ...

Reach up to the ceiling

Reach up to the ceiling,
Bend down to the floor.
Stand up straight
And stretch your arms
Till they will stretch no more.

Bring them in and let them fall,
Then you must bend your knees,
Put your hands above your head,
And do not wobble, PLEASE!

Brick on a brick

You put a brick on a brick and a brick on a brick
To build up a great big wall.
With a brick on a brick and a brick on a brick
You can make it ever so tall.
But you must make sure that the bricks are steady
And firmly fixed to the ground,
For if you're too quick the cement won't stick
And the bricks will all fall down!

Balloon

If you blow and blow and blow
Your balloon will grow and grow.
But if you blow and do not stop –
Your balloon will go off POP!

Funny things I can do

With my feet I can kick, kick, kick,
With my tongue I can lick, lick, lick,
With my fingers I click, click, click,
Oh, funny things I can do!

With my feet I can leap, leap, leap,
With my eyes I can peep, peep, peep,
On my hands I can creep, creep, creep,
Oh, funny things I can do!

Chorus *You can do so many things, simply being you,*
Bumping, jumping, thumping, pumping,
Calling, crawling, bawling, falling,
Just do what you want to do.

With my feet I can skip, skip, skip,
With my lips I can sip, sip, sip,
With my hands I can grip, grip, grip,
Oh, funny things I can do!

Chorus *You can do so many things simply being you,*
Hugging, shrugging, lugging, tugging,
Slapping, tapping, flapping, clapping,
Just do what you want to do.

With my feet I can spring, spring, spring,
With my voice I can sing, sing, sing,
With my hands I can cling, cling, cling,
Oh, funny things I can do,
Funny things I can do!

The teapot

I'm a little teapot, short and stout;
Here's my handle, here's my spout.
When I see the tea-cups, hear me shout,
'Tip me up and pour me out!'

One finger, two fingers

One finger, two fingers, three fingers, four,
Fold them down and make a fist,
Then bang upon the door.

Don't go, Jo!

Don't go, don't go, don't go, Jo!
Can't you see the snow, Jo?
If you put your foot outside
It will freeze your toe, Jo!

This is the way

This is the way to saw a tree,
Saw, saw, saw.
This is the way to pour out tea,
Pour, pour, pour.

This is the way to wipe a plate,
Wipe, wipe, wipe.
This is the way to paint a gate,
Paint, paint, paint.

My friend Sarah

My friend Sarah walks like this...
My friend Sarah talks like this...
My friend Sarah jumps like this...
My friend Sarah bumps like this...
My friend Sarah hops like this...
My friend Sarah STOPS like this...

Teddy bear, teddy bear

Teddy bear, teddy bear, wiggle your toes;
Teddy bear, teddy bear, turn up your nose;
Teddy bear, teddy bear, close your lips;
Teddy bear, teddy bear, smack your hips;
Teddy bear, teddy bear, beat your chest,
Then give a big kiss to the one you love best!

One finger, one thumb, keep moving

One finger, one thumb, keep moving,
One finger, one thumb, keep moving,
One finger, one thumb, keep moving,
We'll all be merry and bright.

One finger, one thumb, one arm, keep moving, *etc.*

One finger, one thumb, one arm, one leg, keep moving, *etc.*

One finger, one thumb, one arm, one leg, one nod of the head, *etc.*

One finger, one thumb, one arm, one leg, one nod of the head, stand up, sit down, *etc.*

One finger, one thumb, one arm, one leg, one nod of the head, stand up, sit down, turn around, keep moving, *etc.*

Can you tell me?

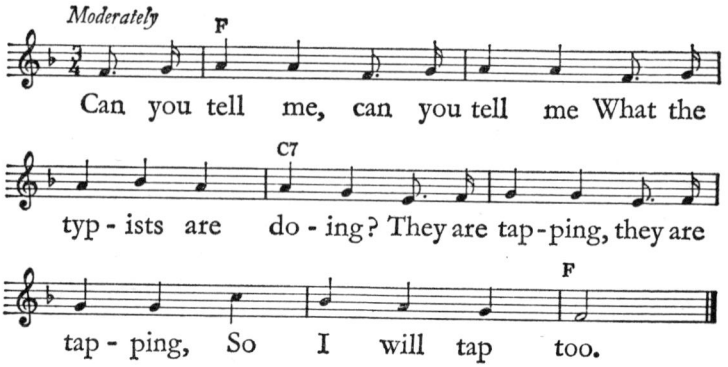

Can you tell me, can you tell me
What the typists are doing?
They are tapping, they are tapping,
So I will tap too.

Can you tell me, can you tell me
What the window cleaners are doing?
They are wiping, they are wiping,
So I will wipe too.

Can you tell me, can you tell me
What the tailors are doing?
They are sewing, they are sewing,
So I will sew too.

Can you tell me, can you tell me
What the pop singers are doing?
They are dancing, they are dancing,
So I will dance too.

Can you tell me, can you tell me
What the grand-dads are doing?
They are nodding, they are nodding,
So I will nod too.

Did you ever see a lassie?

Did you ev-er see a las-sie, A las-sie, a las-sie, Did you ev-er see a las-sie, Go this way and that? Go this way and that way And this way and that way, Did you ev-er see a las-sie Go this way and that?

Did you ever see a lassie,
A lassie, a lassie,
Did you ever see a lassie,
Go this way and that?
Go this way and that way
And this way and that way,
Did you ever see a lassie
Go this way and that?

Did you ever see a laddie? *etc.*

Did you ever see a postman? *etc.*

Did you ever see a policeman? *etc.*

Did you ever see a teacher? *etc.*

Did you ever see a funny clown? *etc.*

If I had a drum...

When I'm on my own
And I don't know what to play,
I look at my toys
And this is what I say –

If I had a drum,
I would beat, beat, beat it.
If I had a cake,
I would eat, eat, eat it.

When I'm on my own
And I don't know what to play,
I look at my toys
And this is what I say –

If I had a ball,
I would throw, throw, throw it.
If I had a boat,
I would row, row, row it.

When I'm on my own
And I don't know what to play,
I look at my toys
And this is what I say –

If I had a pail,
I would fill, fill, fill it.
If I had some water,
I would spill, spill, spill it.

When I'm on my own
And I don't know what to play,
I look at my toys
And this is what I say –

If I had a book,
I would read, read, read it.
If I had a dog,
I would feed, feed, feed it.

What I like to do

Please give me that nail
And I'll knock it in for you.
Knocking in a nail
Is what I like to do.

Please give me that pail
And I'll fill it up for you.
Filling up a pail
Is what I like to do.

Please give me that can
And I'll empty it for you.
Emptying a can
Is what I like to do.

Please give me that pan
And I'll clean it out for you.
Cleaning out a pan
Is what I like to do.

Here we go round the mulberry bush

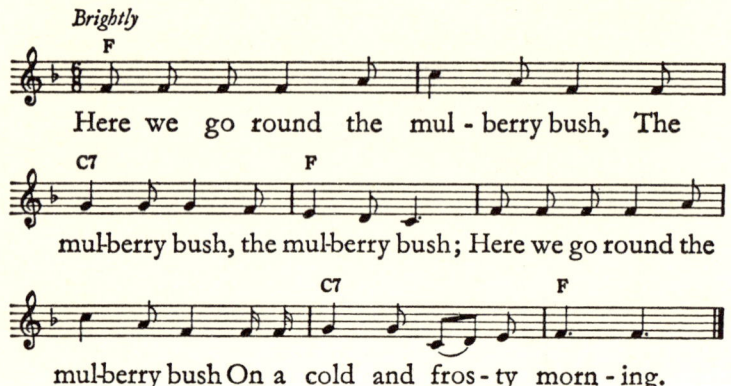

Here we go round the mulberry bush,
The mulberry bush, the mulberry bush;
Her we go round the mulberry bush
On a cold and frosty morning.

This is the way we clap our hands,
Clap our hands, clap our hands;
This is the way we clap our hands
On a cold and frosty morning.

This is the way we brush our shoes . . .

This is the way we wash our face . . .

This is the way we clean our teeth . . .

This is the way we comb our hair . . .

Peter played with one hammer

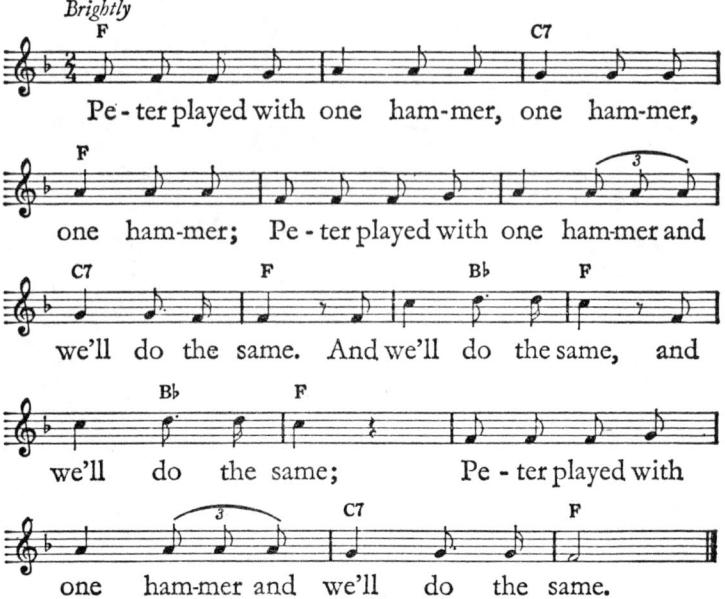

Peter played with one hammer, one hammer, one hammer;
Peter played with one hammer and we'll do the same.
And we'll do the same, and we'll do the same;
Peter played with one hammer and we'll do the same.

Peter played with two hammers . . .

Peter played with three hammers . . .

Peter played with four hammers . . .

Peter played with five hammers . . .

One-eyed Jack and Peg-leg Pete

One-eyed Jack and Peg-leg Pete

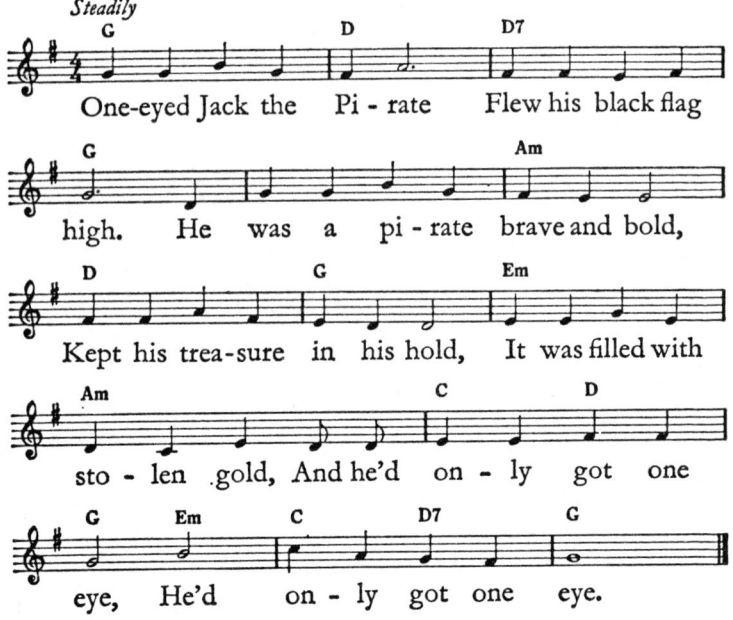

One-eyed Jack the Pirate
Flew his black flag high.
He was a pirate brave and bold,
Kept his treasure in his hold,
It was filled with stolen gold,
And he'd only got one eye,
He'd only got one eye.

Peg-leg Pete the Pirate
Plundered ships at sea.
Kept on firing till they sank,
Made the sailors walk the plank,
Rum and gin were all he drank,
And he'd only got one knee,
He'd only got one knee.

Peg-leg Pete the Pirate
Fought with One-eyed Jack.
They fell into the foaming sea,
A great big whale they didn't see,
And that's the end of our story,
For neither could get back,
No, neither could get back.

Punch and Judy

Punch and Judy
   Fought for a pie,
Punch gave Judy
   A knock in the eye.

Says Punch to Judy,
   'Will you have any more?'
Says Judy to Punch,
   'My eye is too sore.'

Little Boy Blue

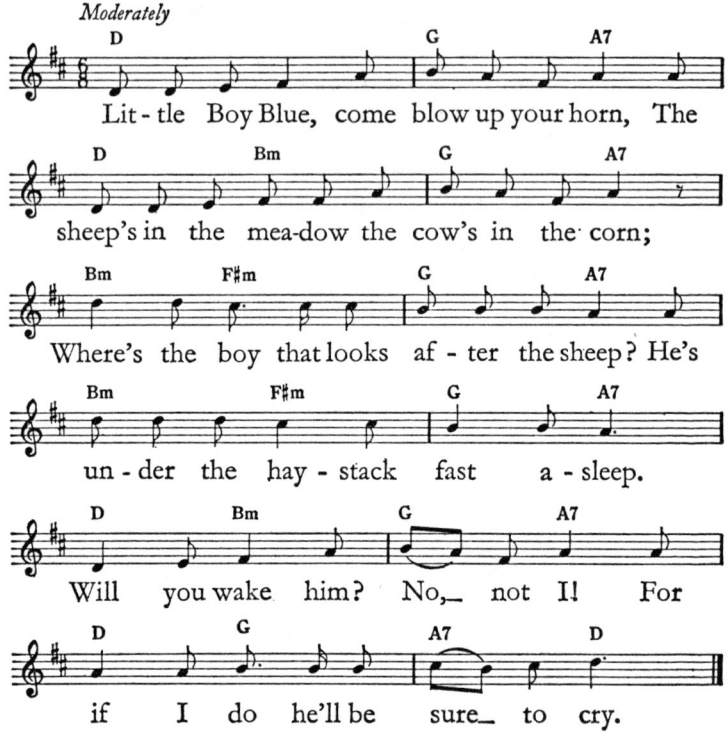

Little Boy Blue, come blow up your horn,
The sheep's in the meadow, the cow's in the corn;
Where's the boy that looks after the sheep?
He's under the haystack fast asleep.
Will you wake him? No, not I!
For if I do he'll be sure to cry.

O, the grand old Duke of York

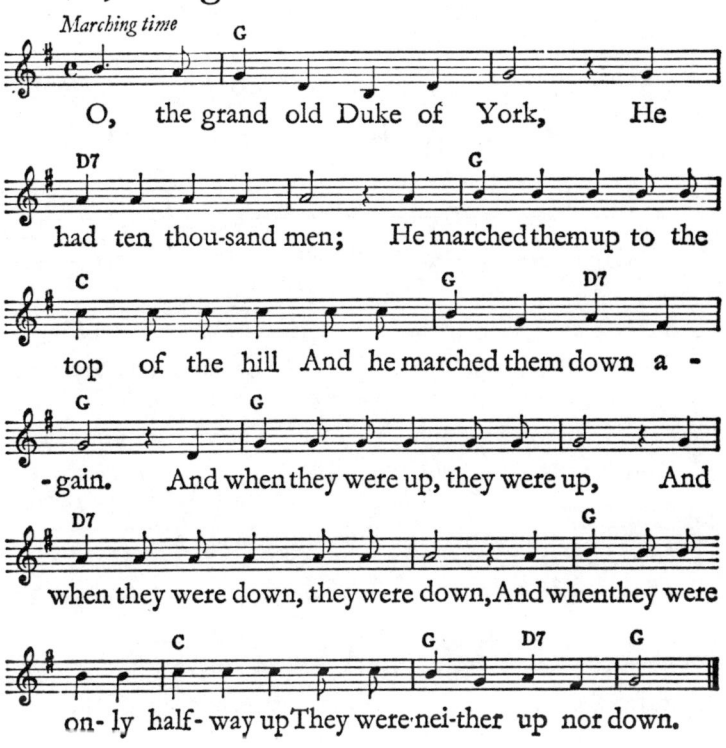

O, the grand old Duke of York,
He had ten thousand men;
He marched them up to the top of the hill
And he marched them down again.
And when they were up, they were up,
And when they were down, they were down,
And when they were only halfway up
They were neither up nor down.

I know an old lady

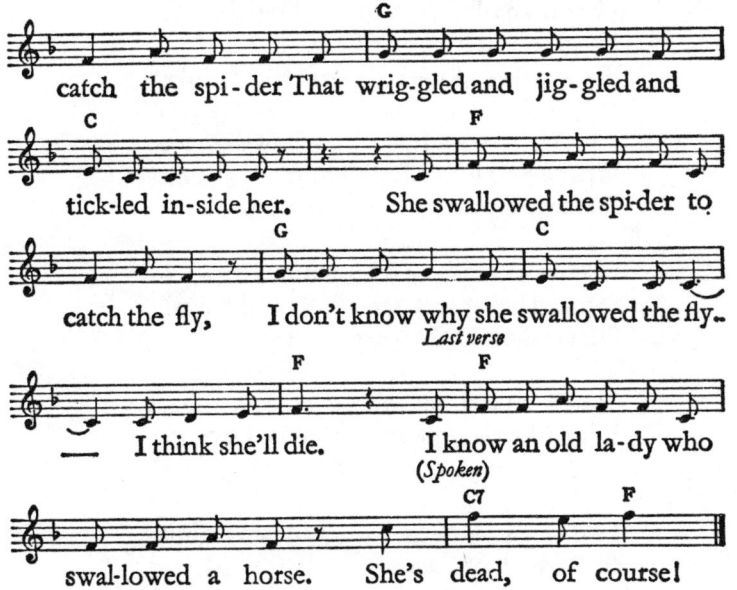

I know an old lady who swallowed a fly.
I don't know why she swallowed a fly.
I think she'll die.

I know an old lady who swallowed a spider
That wriggled and jiggled and tickled inside her.
She swallowed the spider to catch the fly,
I don't know why she swallowed the fly.
I think she'll die.

I know an old lady who swallowed a bird.
How absurd to swallow a bird!
She swallowed the bird to catch the spider
That wriggled and jiggled and tickled inside her.
She swallowed the spider to catch the fly,
I don't know why she swallowed the fly.
I think she'll die.

I know an old lady who swallowed a cat.
Imagine that! She swallowed a cat.
She swallowed the cat to catch the bird *etc.*

I know an old lady who swallowed a dog.
What a hog to swallow a dog!
She swallowed the dog to catch the cat *etc.*

I know an old lady who swallowed a goat.
Opened her throat and swallowed a goat.
She swallowed the goat to catch the dog *etc.*

I know an old lady who swallowed a cow.
I don't know how she swallowed a cow.
She swallowed a cow to catch the goat *etc.*

I know an old lady who swallowed a horse.
She's dead, of course!

Funny Jim

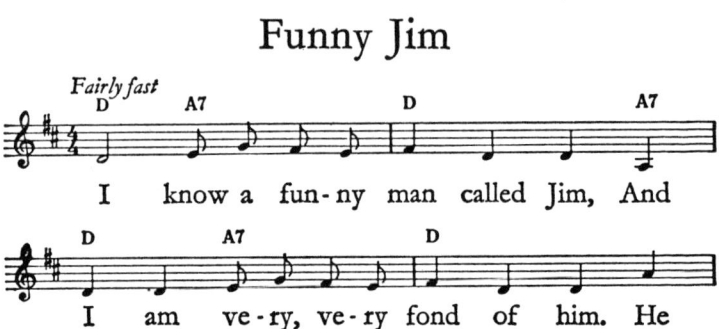

I know a funny man called Jim, And
I am very, very fond of him. He

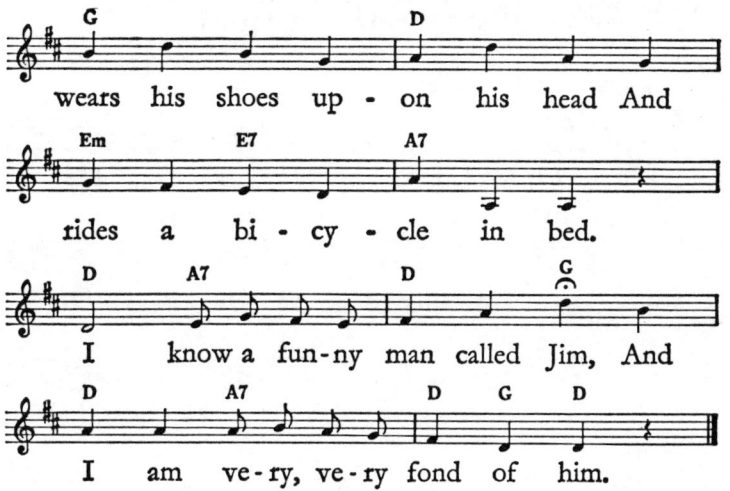

I know a funny man called Jim,
And I am very, very fond of him.
He wears his shoes upon his head
And rides a bicycle in bed.
I know a funny man called Jim,
And I am very, very fond of him.

I know a silly man called Joe
Who likes his weeds to grow and grow.
And he will dig for hours and hours
And take up all his lovely flowers.
I know a silly man called Joe
Who likes his weeds to grow and grow.

I know a nosey man called John
Who has to know whatever's going on.
What you say, what you do,
Nosey John is watching YOU.
I know a nosey man called John
Who has to know whatever's going on.

There was a farmer

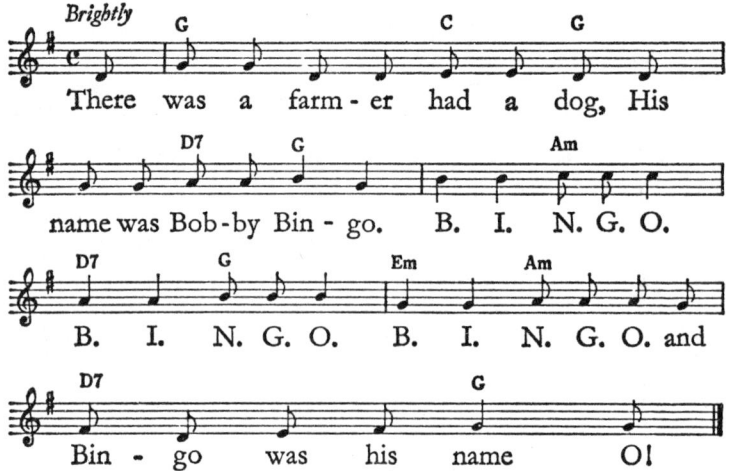

There was a farmer had a dog,
His name was Bobby Bingo.
B.I.N.G.O. B.I.N.G.O.
B.I.N.G.O. and Bingo was his name O!

Diddle, diddle, dumpling, my son John

Did-dle, did-dle, dump-ling, my son John
Went to bed with his breech-es on,
One shoe off and the o-ther shoe on;
Did-dle, did-dle, dump-ling, my son John.

Diddle, diddle, dumpling, my son John
Went to bed with his breeches on,
One shoe off and the other shoe on;
Diddle, diddle, dumpling, my son John.

The robbers

See the robbers passing by,
Passing by, passing by.
See the robbers passing by,
My fair lady.

What have the robbers done to you,
Done to you, done to you?
What have the robbers done to you,
My fair lady?

They broke the lock and stole the key,
Stole the key, stole the key.
They broke the lock and stole the key,
My fair lady.

How many pounds will set you free,
Set you free, set you free?
How many pounds will set you free,
My fair lady?

Twenty pounds will set me free,
Set me free, set me free.
Twenty pounds will set me free,
My fair lady.

So much money I have not got,
Have not got, have not got.
So much money I have not got,
My fair lady.

Then off to prison you must go,
You must go, you must go.
Then off to prison you must go,
My fair lady.

Little Bo-Peep

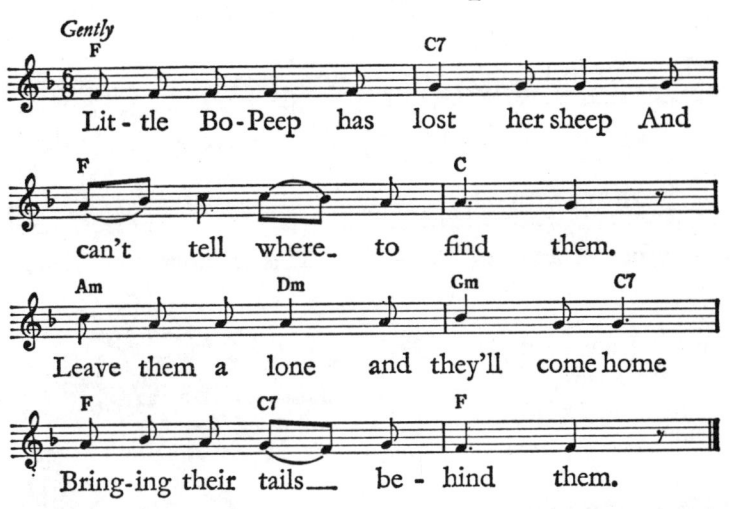

Little Bo-Peep has lost her sheep
And can't tell where to find them.
Leave them alone and they'll come home
Bringing their tails behind them.

When I was a lady

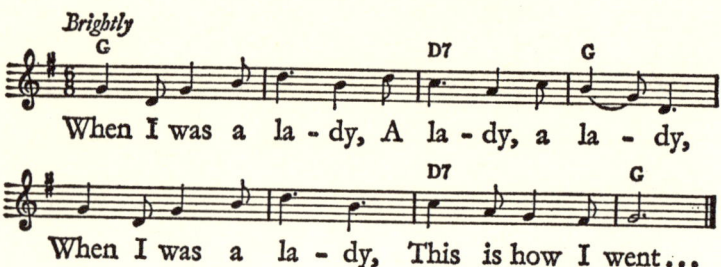

When I was a la-dy, A la-dy, a la-dy,
When I was a la-dy, This is how I went...

When I was a lady,
A lady, a lady,
When I was a lady,
This is how I went ...

When I was a farmer,
A farmer, a farmer,
When I was a farmer,
This is how I went ...

When I was a princess,
A princess, a princess,
When I was a princess,
This is how I went ...

When Jacky's a very good boy

When Jacky's a very good boy
   He shall have cakes and a custard,
But when he does nothing but cry,
   He shall have nothing but mustard.

If I were a king

If I were a king
I would wear a crown of gold,
And all the people round me
Would do as they were told.

If I were a queen
I would have a golden bed,
And there I'd eat my breakfast
With my crown upon my head.

If you should meet a giant

If you should meet a giant,
Don't say: 'You're very tall,'
Or he might take you in his hand
And say: '*You're* very small!'

The chimney sweep

Swee–ep! Swee–ep! Swee–ep! Swee–ep!

Here comes Joe the chimney sweep,
Black as coal from head to feet.
When the children see him coming,
Down the street they all start running;
Calling, calling, Swee–ep! Swee–ep!
Here comes Joe the chimney sweep.

Jack and Jill

Marching time

Jack and Jill went up the hill To fetch a pail of wa-ter. Jack fell down and broke his crown, And Jill came tumb-ling af-ter.

Jack and Jill went up the hill
To fetch a pail of water.
Jack fell down and broke his crown,
And Jill came tumbling after.

Up Jack got and home did trot
As fast as he could caper.
He went to bed to mend his head
With vinegar and brown paper.

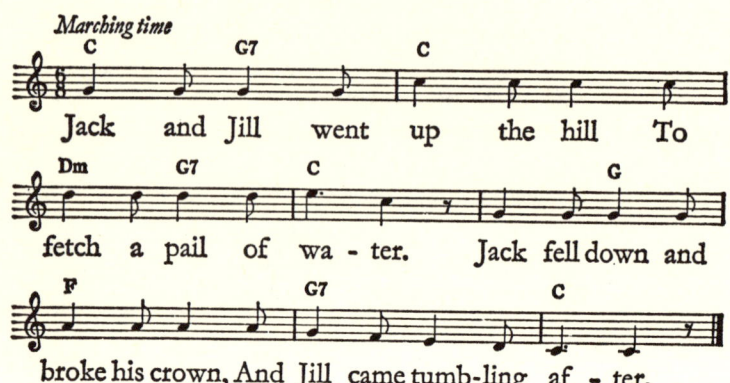

The policeman

Watch the policeman in the street
Move his arms but not his feet;
He only has to raise his hand,
Cars and buses understand.
He can make them stop and go,
He can move them to and fro.
Watch the policeman in the street
Move his arms but not his feet.

Five little boys

Five little boys were playing on the shore;
A pirate captured one and then there were four.

Four little boys were swimming in the sea;
A shark showed its teeth and then there were three.

Three little boys cried: 'Who's afraid of you?'
When a whale came along and then there were two.

Two little boys began to shout and run;
A big wave crashed and then there was one.

One little boy said: 'I'm the only one.'
So he ran home to tea and then there were none.

What are little boys made of?

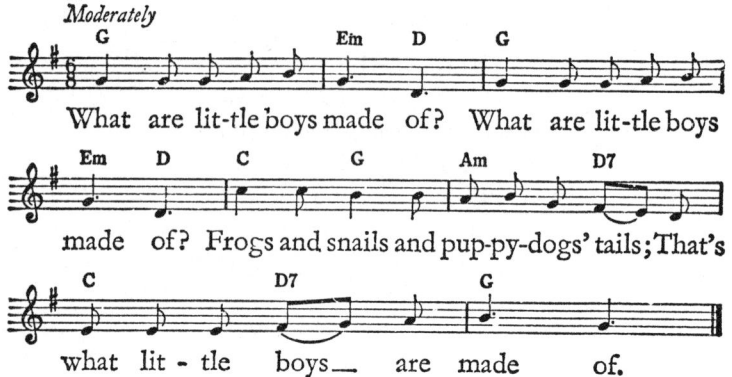

What are little boys made of?
What are little boys made of?
Frogs and snails and puppy-dogs' tails;
That's what little boys are made of.

What are little girls made of?
What are little girls made of?
Sugar and spice and all things nice;
That's what little girls are made of.

Humpty Dumpty

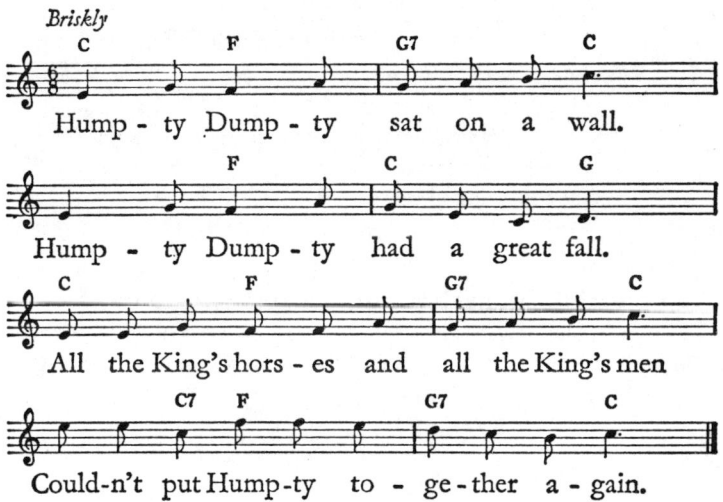

Humpty Dumpty sat on a wall.
Humpty Dumpty had a great fall.
All the King's horses and all the King's men
Couldn't put Humpty together again.

The witch's broomstick

The witch has lost her broomstick and can't fly in the sky,
The witch has lost her broomstick and only I know why.
The witch has lost her broomstick and someone else will fly,
And I know who that someone is – it's I, I, I!

Teddy lost his coat

Teddy lost his coat,
Teddy lost his hat,
Teddy lost his rubber boots –
What do you think of that?

Teddy found his coat,
Teddy found his hat,
Teddy found his rubber boots –
He'd left them on the MAT!

Two little eyes

Two little eyes to look around,
Two little ears to hear each sound,
One little nose to smell what's sweet,
One little mouth that likes to eat.

The little hunter

There was a little hunter
Went looking for a hare,
And where he hoped the hare would be
He found a hairy bear!

'Good afternoon,' said hairy bear,
'I'm very glad you came.'
The hunter turned head-over-heels
And hurried home again!

Little Miss Muffet

Little Miss Muffet sat on a tuffet,
Eating her curds and whey.
There came a big spider
And sat down beside her,
And frightened Miss Muffet away.

The farmer's in his den

The farmer's in his den,
The farmer's in his den,
Hey-ho my daddy oh,
The farmer's in his den.

The farmer wants a wife . . .

The wife wants a child . . .

The child wants a nurse . . .

The nurse wants a dog . . .

The dog wants a bone . . .

We all pat the dog . . .

Tommy was a soldier

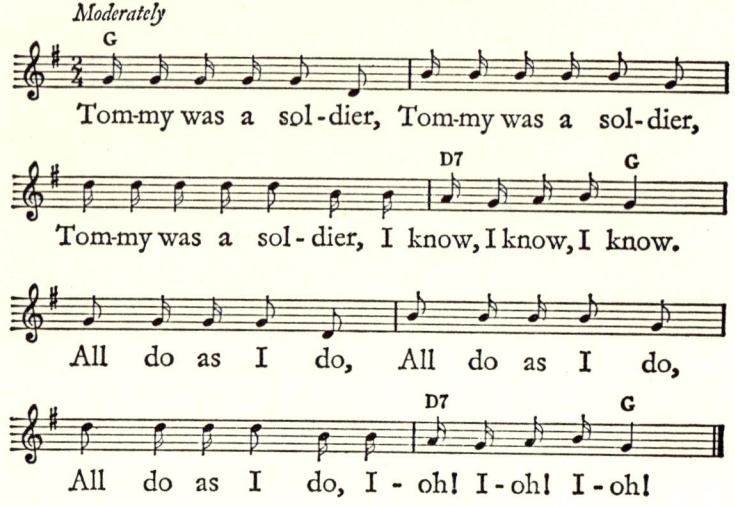

Tommy was a soldier,
Tommy was a soldier,
Tommy was a soldier,
I know, I know, I know.

Chorus *All do as I do,*
All do as I do,
All do as I do,
I-oh! I-oh! I-oh!

Tommy was a policeman ...

Tommy was a postman ...

Tommy was a milkman ...

Tommy was an airman ...

Little Polly Flinders

Little Polly Flinders
Sat among the cinders
Warming her pretty little toes;
Her mother came and caught her,
And smacked her little daughter
For spoiling her nice new clothes.

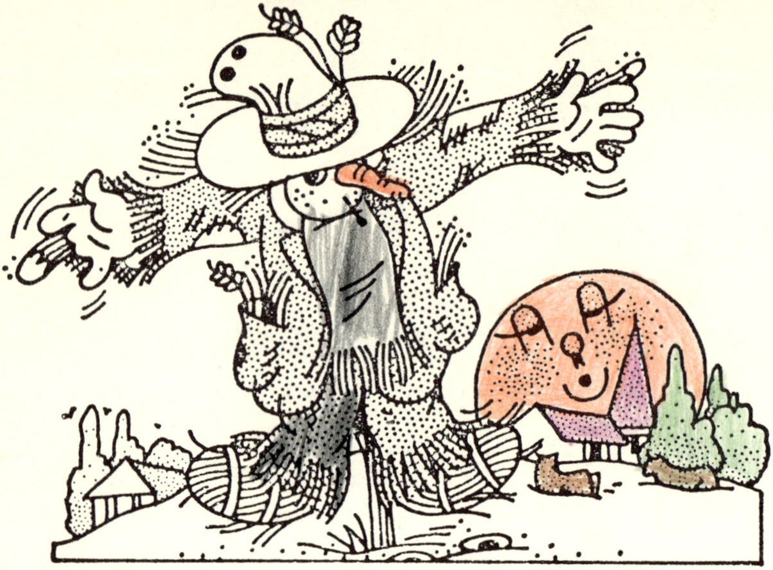

When all the cows were sleeping

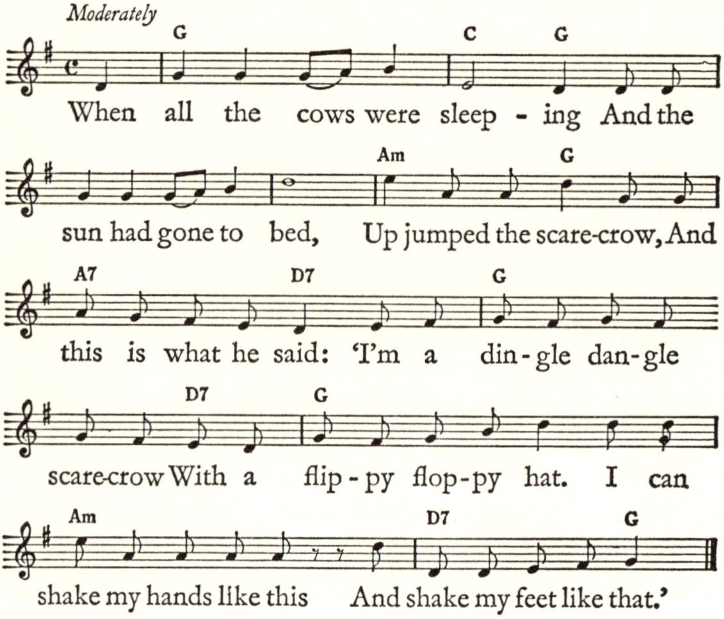

Moderately
G C G
When all the cows were sleep - ing And the
Am G
sun had gone to bed, Up jumped the scare-crow, And
A7 D7 G
this is what he said: 'I'm a din-gle dan-gle
D7 G
scare-crow With a flip-py flop-py hat. I can
Am D7 G
shake my hands like this And shake my feet like that.'

When all the cows were sleeping
And the sun had gone to bed,
Up jumped the scarecrow,
And this is what he said:

'I'm a dingle dangle scarecrow
With a flippy floppy hat.
I can shake my hands like this
And shake my feet like that.'

When all the hens were roosting
And the moon was round and bright,
Up jumped the scarecrow
And cried with all his might:

'I'm a dingle dangle scarecrow
With a flippy floppy hat.
I can shake my hands like this
And shake my feet like that.'

Isabella Perkins

Isabella Perkins
Lost her little cat.
She looked for her and found her
Asleep in Daddy's hat.

Ebenezer Perkins
Lost his nanny goat.
He looked for her and found her
Wrapped up in Daddy's coat.

Cousin Peter

Last evening Cousin Peter came, Last evening Cousin Peter came, Last evening Cousin Peter came To show that he was here.

Last evening Cousin Peter came,
Last evening Cousin Peter came,
Last evening Cousin Peter came
To show that he was here.

He knocked three times upon the door ...

He wiped his feet upon the mat ...

He hung his hat upon the hook ...

He kicked his shoes off one by one ...

He danced about in stocking feet ...

He tossed us up into the air ...

He played he was a great big bear ...

He made a bow and said goodbye,
He made a bow and said goodbye,
He made a bow and said goodbye
To show that he was gone.

Two fat gentlemen

Two fat gentlemen met in a lane,
Bowed most politely, bowed once again.
How do you do?
How do you do?
And how do you do again.

Two tall policemen ...

Two busy postmen ...

Two thin ladies ...

Two big schoolboys ...

Two fierce tigers ...

Two hungry lions ...

There was a crooked man

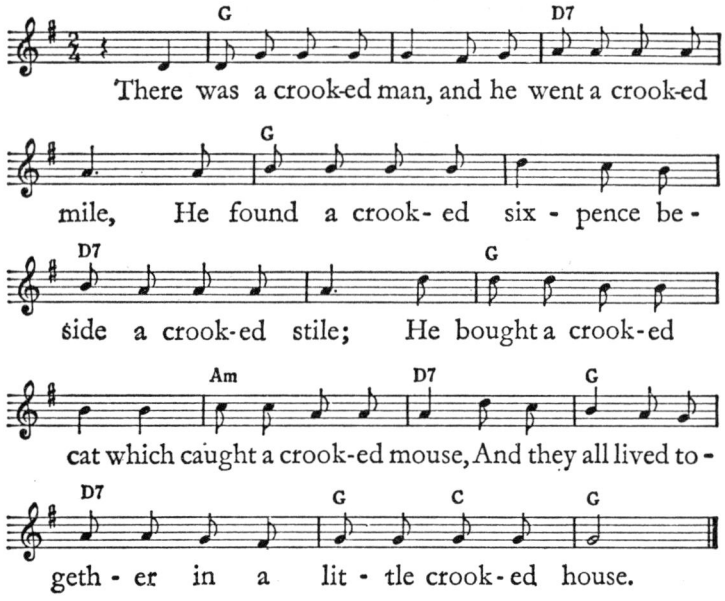

There was a crooked man, and he went a crooked mile,
He found a crooked sixpence beside a crooked stile;
He bought a crooked cat which caught a crooked mouse,
And they all lived together in a little crooked house.

Here's a church

Here's a church,
Here's a steeple.
Open the door
And out come the people.

One man went to mow

One man went to mow,
Went to mow a meadow;
One man and his dog
Went to mow a meadow.

Two men went to mow,
Went to mow a meadow;
Two men, one man and his dog
Went to mow a meadow.

Three men went to mow,
Went to mow a meadow;
Three men, two men, one man and his dog
Went to mow a meadow.

A little man is standing

A little man is standing among the trees.
He wears a scarlet coat down to his knees.
If you know, then you tell me what this little man can be,
Standing still and lonesome there among the trees.

Lay the cloth

Lay the cloth, knife and fork,
Bring me up a leg of pork.
If it's lean bring it in,
If it's fat take it back,
Tell the old woman I don't want that!

Adam and Eve and Pinch-me

Adam and Eve and Pinch-me
Went down to the river to bathe;
Adam and Eve were drowned,
Who do you think was saved?

The ghostesses

There were three ghostesses
Sitting on postesses
Eating buttered toastesses
And greasing their fistesses
Right up to their wristesses.
Weren't they beastesses
To make such feastesses?

John Brown had a little guinea-pig

John Brown had a little guinea-pig,
John Brown had a little guinea-pig,
John Brown had a little guinea-pig,
One little guinea-pig.

There was one little, two little, three little guinea-pigs,
Four little, five little, six little guinea-pigs,
Seven little, eight little, nine little guinea-pigs,
Ten little guinea-pigs.

Sam, Sam, dirty old man

Sam, Sam, dirty old man,
Washed his face in a frying pan,
Combed his hair with a donkey's tail
And scratched his tummy with his big toenail.

Queen, Queen, Caroline

Queen, Queen, Caroline,
Washed her head in turpentine,
Turpentine to make it shine.
Queen, Queen, Caroline.

Old King Cole

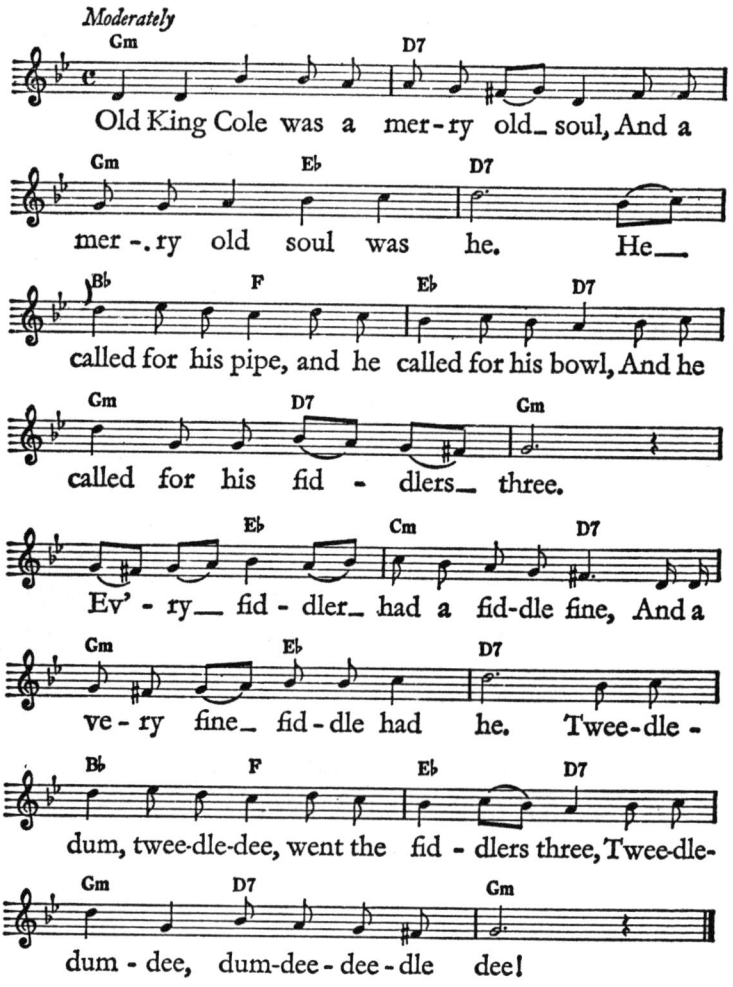

Old King Cole was a merry old soul,
　　And a merry old soul was he.
He called for his pipe, and he called for his bowl,
　　And he called for his fiddlers three.
Ev'ry fiddler had a fiddle fine,
　　And a very fine fiddle had he.
Tweedle dum, tweedledee, went the fiddlers three,
　　Tweedledum-dee, dum-dee-dee-dle dee!

Old King Cole was a merry old soul,
　　And a merry old soul was he.
He called for his pipe, and he called for his bowl,
　　And he called for his harpers three.
Ev'ry harper had a fine harp,
　　And a very fine harp had he,
Twang-a-twang, twang-a-twang, went the harpers three,
　　Twang-a-twang, twang, twang-a-twang-a twee.

Old King Cole was a merry old soul,
　　And a merry old soul was he.
He called for his pipe, and he called for his bowl,
　　And he called for his drummers three.
Ev'ry drummer had a fine drum,
　　And a very fine drum had he,
Rub-a-dub, rub-a-dub, went the
　　　　　　　　drummers three,
Rub-a-dub, dub, rub-a-dub-a dee.

Index

Adam and Eve and Pinch-me (*Trad.*) 213
Aeroplanes, aeroplanes (*B.I.*) 81
A frog went walking on a summer's day (*Trad.*) 18
A little boy went into a barn (*Trad.*) 41
A little man is standing among the trees (*Trad.*) 212
A little rabbit on a hill (*Trad.*) 139
At seven o'clock the milkman comes (*B.I.*) 58
Baa, Baa black sheep (*Trad.*) 25
Bang! bang! bang! (*B.I.*) 95
Bells are ringing (*Trad.*) 102
Bobby Shafto's gone to sea (*Trad.*) 120
Boom off! (*B.I.*) 123
Bought me a cat (*Trad.*) 96
Bye Baby Bunting (*Trad.*) 72
Can you tell me (*Anon.*) 172
Chook, chook, chook, chook, chook (*Trad.*) 44
Clap your hands together like this (*Trad.*) 151
Clickety-clack and clickety-click (*B.I.*) 81
Clickety-click and clickety-clack (*B.I.*) 81
Come down to the station (*B.I.*) 86
Crash, bang, rattle, boom, boom! (*Trad.*) 110
Dance to your daddy (*Trad.*) 162
Diddle, diddle, dumpling, my son John (*Trad./C.R.*) 191
Did you ever go fishing? (*Trad.*) 158
Did you ever see a lassie? (*Trad.*) 174
Don't go, don't go, don't go, Jo! (*B.I.*) 169
Don't scold so, Susie (*Trad.*) 104
Down among the lilies (*Trad.*) 145
Dring! dring! (*B.I.*) 91
Early in the morning (*B.I.*) 82
Eency, weency spider (*Trad.*) 17
Eight o'clock (*B.I. & C.R.*) 60
Farmer Brown drove into town (*C.R.*) 50
Father and Mother and Big Brother John (*Trad.*) 66
Five fingers wriggling, wriggling (*Trad.*) 144
Five little boys were playing on the shore (*B.I.*) 197
Five little ducks swam out one day (*B.I.*) 80
Five little kittens crept out one day (*Trad.*) 139

Five little ladies sitting in a row (*Trad.*) 140
Five pigeons sitting on a wall (*C.R.*) 30
Foxy's running with a sack (*Trad.*) 154
From Wibbleton to Wobbleton is fifteen miles (*Trad./C.R.*) 116
Going up the hill (*C.R.*) 129
Hands are cold and feet are cold (*Trad.*) 148
Hands clap (*Trad.*) 144
Handy-Spandy, Jack-a-Dandy (*Trad.*) 159
Have you seen the boat leave? (*B.I.*) 93
Hello, hello, hello, sir (*Trad.*) 99
Here's a church (*Trad.*) 210
Here we come gathering nuts in May (*Trad.*) 146
Here we go Looby Loo (*Trad.*) 152
Here we go round the mulberry bush (*Trad.*) 178
Here we plant our beans in a row (*Trad.*) 149
Hey diddle diddle (*Trad.*) 24
Hickory dickory dock (*Trad.*) 54
Hop a little (*B.I./C.R.*) 155
Humpty Dumpty sat on a wall (*Trad.*) 199
Huntsman got up very early (*Trad.*) 147
Hushabye Baby, on the tree top (*Trad.*) 78
Hush, hush, hush (*B.I.*) 82
I am a music man (*Trad.*) 100
If I could walk on the ceiling (*C.R.*) 44
If I had a donkey (*Trad.*) 10
If I were a king (*B.I.*) 195
If you blow and blow and blow (*B.I.*) 165
If you can hear a spoon stirring (*B.I.*) 90
If you should ever need a hole (*B.I.*) 24
If you should meet a giant (*B.I.*) 195
If you take a piece of wood (*C.R.*) 138
If you want to do as I do (*Trad.*) 163
I had a little brother (*Trad.*) 95
I know a funny man called Jim (*B.I./C.R.*) 188
I know an old lady who swallowed a fly (*Trad.*) 186
I like breakfast time (*C.R.*) 48
I like noise (*Anon.*) 103
I like to hike (*B.I.*) 130
I love little pussy (*Trad.*) 33
I'm a clock on the wall (*C.R.*) 46
I'm a lion in the forest (*B.I.*) 32

I'm a little teapot (*Trad.*) 168
I'm alone in the house (*B.I./C.R.*) 88
I'm a pet (*B.I.*) 15
'I'm going to sleep,' said Tired Ben (*B.I.*) 52
Into the basin put the plums (*Trad.*) 140
Isabella Perkins (*B.I.*) 207
I saw three boats come sailing by (*C.R.*) 126
I scream (*Trad.*) 86
I've got a secret friend (*B.I.*) 67
I've got five trees standing in a row (*C.R.*) 160
I walked across the farmyard (*B.I.*) 111
I walked to the top of the hill (*B.I./C.R.*) 161
I went for a walk in the park today (*B.I.*) 36
I went to the cupboard (*B.I.*) 62
I wish I were a lamb in the field (*B.I./C.R.*) 16
Jack and Jill went up the hill (*Trad.*) 196
Jack be nimble (*Trad.*) 147
Jelly and cream (*C.R.*) 64
Jelly in the bowl (*B.I.*) 158
Jingle bells (*Trad.*) 106
John Brown had a little guinea-pig (*B.I./Trad.*) 214
Knock, knock at the door (*Trad.*) 145
Ladybird, ladybird, fly away home! (*Trad.*) 14
Last evening Cousin Peter came (*Trad.*) 208
Lay the cloth, knife and fork (*Trad.*) 213
Lazy Mary, will you get up? (*Trad.*) 52
Let's go to the seaside (*B.I.*) 130
Little Bo-Peep has lost her sheep (*Trad.*) 193
Little Boy Blue, come blow up your horn (*Trad.*) 184
Little man, little man (*B.I.*) 9
Little Miss Muffet sat on a tuffet (*Trad.*) 202
Little Robin Redbreast (*Trad.*) 10
Little Polly Flinders (*Trad.*) 205
Little Robin Redbreast sat upon a tree (*Trad.*) 41
Look at your hat! (*B.I.*) 63
Monday, Tuesday, Wednesday (*B.I.*) 68
My friend Sarah walks like this (*B.I.*) 170
My Mummy is a Mummy (*B.I.*) 66
My shoes were too small (*B.I.*) 73
My sister in the garden (*B.I.*) 90
Oh dear, what can the matter be? (*Trad.*) 56

Oh – we can play on the big bass drum *(Trad.)* 105
Oh, you push the damper in *(Trad.)* 141
Old King Cole was a merry old soul *(Trad.)* 216
One elephant went out to play *(Trad.)* 40
One-eyed Jack the Pirate *(B.I./C.R.)* 182
One finger, one thumb, keep moving *(Trad.)* 171
One finger, two fingers, three fingers, four *(B.I.)* 169
One is one and two is two *(B.I.)* 119
One little bugler coming from the war *(Trad.)* 94
One little cockerel, bright and gay *(Trad.)* 107
One man went to mow *(Trad.)* 211
'Oranges and lemons,' say the bells of St Clements *(Trad.)* 108
O, the grand old Duke of York *(Trad.)* 185
O where, O where has my little dog gone? *(Trad.)* 8
Peter played with one hammer *(Trad.)* 180
Playtime, playtime *(B.I.)* 57
Please give me that nail *(B.I.)* 177
Polly put the kettle on *(Trad.)* 65
Punch and Judy *(Trad.)* 183
Push with your feet and pedal fast *(B.I.)* 158
Pussy-cat, pussy-cat, where have you been? *(Trad.)* 127
Put out your arm and touch the wall *(B.I./C.R.)* 143
Queen, Queen, Caroline *(Trad.)* 215
Rain, rain, go away *(Trad.)* 150
Rap, rap, rap went the window-cleaning man *(B.I.)* 114
Rat a tat tat, who is that? *(Trad.)* 32
Reach up to the ceiling *(B.I.)* 163
Ride a cock horse to Banbury Cross *(Trad.)* 98
Ring-a-ring-o'-roses *(Trad.)* 83
Round and round the village *(Trad.)* 137
Sam, Sam, dirty old man *(Trad.)* 215
See-saw, Margery Daw *(Trad.)* 142
See the robbers passing by *(Trad.)* 192
Sheep, sheep, come home! *(B.I.)* 22
Show me what you've got in your hand *(B.I./C.R.)* 70
Sing a song of sixpence *(Trad.)* 27
Sing a song of spaceships *(B.I./Trad.)* 122
Sing a song of work to do *(B.I./C.R.)* 74
Sitting on a pony, riding into town *(C.R.)* 128
Six little ducks that I once knew *(Trad.)* 37
Smell a rose *(B.I.)* 150

Spinning-wheel go round and round (*Trad.*) 87
Susie Simpkin went to France (*Trad.*) 159
Swee-ep! Swee-ep! Swee-ep! (*Trad.*) 195
Teddy bear, Teddy bear wiggle your toes (*B.I.*) 170
Teddy lost his coat (*B.I.*) 201
Ten fat sausages frying in the pan (*Trad.*) 84
Ten galloping horses came to town (*Trad.*) 123
The animals went in two by two (*Trad.*) 42
The bear went over the mountain (*Trad.*) 34
The big brown hen and Mrs Duck (*Trad.*) 102
The big ship sails through the ally, ally O (*Trad.*) 125
The buses and the motor cars (*C.R.*) 130
The clock stands still (*B.I.*) 55
The dog was on the log (*C.R.*) 15
The farmer's in his den (*Trad.*) 203
The lion is king of the jungle (*C.R.*) 20
The Milkman comes with a clinkety-clink (*C.R.*) 92
The north wind doth blow (*Trad.*) 26
The postman raps hard (*B.I.*) 90
There isn't time (*B.I.*) 53
There's a fox in a box in my little bed (*B.I./C.R.*) 12
There's music in a hammer (*Trad.*) 93
There was a crooked man (*Trad.*) 210
There was a farmer had a dog (*Trad.*) 190
There was a little dog (*Trad.*) 153
There was a little hunter (*Trad.*) 201
There was a small maiden named Maggie (*Trad.*) 14
There were four jolly country men (*C.R.*) 132
There were three ghostesses (*Trad.*) 213
There were two little dickey birds (*Trad.*) 11
The saucepan lids went clang (*B.I.*) 99
The wheels on the bus go round and round (*Trad.*) 131
The witch has lost her broomstick (*B.I./C.R.*) 200
This is the way (*B.I.*) 169
This little pig went to market (*Trad.*) 9
This old man, he played one (*Trad.*) 112
This red balloon that I've got in my hand (*B.I.*) 118
Three blind mice (*Trad.*) 29
Through the teeth (*Trad.*) 159
Time and time again (*B.I./C.R.*) 59
Time is fun (*B.I.*) 55

Tip-toe, tip-toe (*B.I.*) 71
To market, to market, to buy a fat pig (*Trad.*) 117
Tommy was a soldier (*Trad.*) 204
Tooting and hooting, tooting and hooting (*B.I.*) 93
Two clean hands (*Trad.*) 144
Two fat gentlemen met in a lane (*Trad.*) 209
Two little eyes to look around (*Trad.*) 201
Up and down, high and low (*C.R.*) 156
Up in the North, a long way off (*Trad.*) 10
Watch the policeman in the street (*C.R.*) 197
We all get up at seven (*B.I.*) 53
We'll all clap hands together (*Trad.*) 136
What are little boys made of? (*Trad.*) 198
What's inside my big brown basket? (*B.I.*) 73
What's the time? (*B.I.*) 58
When all the cows were sleeping (*Trad.*) 206
When I get dressed I put my vest on (*C.R.*) 76
When I look into the looking-glass (*B.I.*) 62
When I'm on my own (*B.I.*) 176
When I was a lady (*Trad./C.R.*) 194
When Jacky's a very good boy (*Trad.*) 194
Where have you been? (*B.I.*) 9
Who killed Cock Robin? (*Trad.*) 38
Willy Boy, Willy Boy, where are you going? (*B.I.*) 124
With my feet I can kick, kick, kick (*C.R.*) 166
Would you dare, would you dare? (*B.I.*) 28
You can go to sleep on a train (*B.I.*) 118
You put a brick on a brick (*C.R.*) 164